Zara Mustafa

The New Silk Road Kitchen

Ancient Flavors, Modern Healthy Indian, Pakistani & Afghani Recipes for Your Air Fryer, Slow Cooker & Juicer

Copyright © 2025 by Zara Mustafa
All rights reserved.

No part of this publication may be reproduced, distributed, or transmitted in any form or by any means, including photocopying, recording, or other electronic or mechanical methods, without the prior written permission of the publisher, except in the case of brief quotations embodied in critical reviews and certain other noncommercial uses permitted by copyright law.

Illustrations and Design: MK Storyworks
Publisher: MK Storyworks
ISBN: 978-1-80700-010-3

First Edition, 2025

The recipes, techniques, and tips in this book are based on the author's personal experience and research. The author and publisher assume no responsibility for any adverse effects or consequences resulting from the use of the information contained herein.

The New Silk Road Kitchen
by Zara Mustafa

TABLE OF CONTENTS

Air Fryer (The Modern Tandoor)

- Afghani 'Bolani' (Crispy Stuffed Flatbread)
- Air Fryer Peshawari Chapli Kebabs
- Air Fryer 'Shahi Tukda' (Crisped Bread in Saffron Milk)
- Air Fryer Tandoori Chicken Tikka
- Banjan Borani (Afghani Silky Eggplant with Yogurt)
- Crispy Onion & Spinach Pakoras
- Lahori 'Fried' Fish
- Spiced Cauliflower 'Steaks'
- Tandoori-Style Paneer & Pepper Skewers

Slow Cooker (The Patient Pot)

- Afghani Chicken & Apricot Korma
- Hearty Rajma (Indian Kidney Bean Curry)
- Simplified Chicken Haleem
- Slow Cooker Lahori Chana Masala
- Slow Cooker Lamb Shank Nihari
- 'Zero-Ghee' Slow Cooker Daal Makhani

Juices & Sharbat

- Afghani Pomegranate & Rose Elixir
- 'Badam Doodh' (Healthy Saffron & Cardamom Almond Milk)
- Khyber Cucumber & Mint Cooler
- Pink 'Noon' Chai (Simplified Kashmiri Chai)
- Spiced 'Shikanji' (Digestive Cumin Lemonade)
- The "Golden Glow" Mango Turmeric Lassi

TABLE OF CONTENTS

Stovetop (Sabzi, Mains & Grains)

- Aloo Gobi (Without the Mush)
- Bhindi Masala (Quick Okra Stir-Fry)
- Light & Quick Palak Paneer
- Quinoa Pulao with Peas & Cashews
- Simplified Weeknight Kabuli Pulao
- Tadka Daal (20-Minute Yellow Lentil Soup)
- The Perfect, Fluffy Basmati Rice

Companions (Chutneys, Raitas & Breads)

- Avocado, Mint & Cilantro Chutney
- Afghani 'Chakkah' (Strained Garlic & Mint Yogurt)
- Cucumber & Cumin Raita
- Simple Whole-Wheat Roti
- Sirke Waale Pyaaz (Quick-Pickled Vinegar Onions)
- Sweet & Tangy Date and Tamarind Chutney

Sweets (Light & Fragrant)

- Air Fryer 'Shahi Tukda'
- Almond-Flour Besan Barfi
- Date & Fig 'Laddoo' (5-Minute Energy Balls)
- Mango & Coconut Chia Seed Pudding
- Rose Water & Pistachio 'Nice Cream'
- Saffron & Cardamom Panna Cotta

TABLE OF CONTENTS

By Main Ingredient

Chicken & Lamb

- Afghani Chicken & Apricot Korma
- Air Fryer Peshawari Chapli Kebabs (can use chicken)
- Air Fryer Tandoori Chicken Tikka
- Simplified Chicken Haleem
- Simplified Weeknight Kabuli Pulao (uses chicken)
- Slow Cooker Lamb Shank Nihari

Fish

- Lahori 'Fried' Fish

Vegetarian & Plant-Based

- Afghani 'Bolani' (Stuffed Flatbread)
- Aloo Gobi (Potato & Cauliflower)
- Banjan Borani (Eggplant with Yogurt)
- Bhindi Masala (Okra Stir-Fry)
- Crispy Onion & Spinach Pakoras
- Hearty Rajma (Kidney Bean Curry)
- Light & Quick Palak Paneer
- Quinoa Pulao with Peas & Cashews
- Slow Cooker Lahori Chana Masala (Chickpea Curry)
- Spiced Cauliflower 'Steaks'
- Tadka Daal (Yellow Lentil Soup)
- Tandoori-Style Paneer & Pepper Skewers
- 'Zero-Ghee' Slow Cooker Daal Makhani (Black Lentil Curry)
- (All Raitas, Chutneys, Breads, and Sweets can be vegetarian. Many are vegan or easily adapted.)

Dedication

For my grandmothers, Daadi and Naani, who saw no borders in their kitchens, only family. And for my children, that they may inherit the full, undivided flavor of their heritage.

Author's Note
(The Story of This Food)

My childhood was a delicious map.

My father's chapli kebabs tasted of the rugged, smoky air of Peshawar. My mother's daal was pure Delhi, bright with turmeric and sizzling with a cumin tadka. And on special occasions, my aunt would bring over Kabuli Pulao, a fragrant, jeweled rice that tasted, to me, like a faraway kingdom.

My family is a beautiful, complicated tapestry woven from the threads of Afghanistan, Pakistan, and India. But in our kitchen, the borders that men drew on maps vanished. The food was one story, a shared history of Mughal courts, mountain passes, and bustling spice markets.

But as I grew older and built my own life, I found that the food I loved didn't always love me back. The recipes from my grandmothers, written in their hearts, were from an era of hard, physical labor. They were rich, heavy, and time-consuming, swimming in glorious pools of ghee and oil.

I was a modern woman with a busy life, a full-time job, and a desire to feel light and energetic. I refused to accept that to be "healthy," I had to give up the food of my ancestors. I refused to believe that my heritage was incompatible with my wellness.

This book is the result of a long, delicious journey to reclaim my food.

I realized the answer wasn't in my grandmother's heavy-bottomed kadhai; it was on my countertop. My air fryer became my new tandoor, crisping pakoras and tikkas to perfection with just a whisper of oil. My slow cooker became my trusted degh, simmering a Nihari or Daal Makhani for eight hours, building a depth of flavor that once took a full day of watching the stove.

The New Silk Road Kitchen is not about "diet" food. It is about smart food. It's about honoring tradition by making it sustainable for our lives today

Here, you will find the crispy, spicy, tangy joy of a Lahori fried fish, but made in 15 minutes in the air fryer. You will find the creamy, soul-soothing comfort of an Afghani Korma, lightened with yogurt and cashews instead of heavy cream. You will find vibrant juices and sharp, bright salads that cut through the richness.

This is my food. This is our food. It is ancient, and it is new. It is the story of three great cultures, united on a single, healthy plate.

Welcome to my kitchen.

Zara Mustafa

CHAPTER 1

The New Silk Road Pantry

Welcome to my pantry. This is where the magic happens, and I promise you, it's not as complicated as it looks.

If you're new to these cuisines, a list of "essential" spices can feel like a barrier to entry. I want you to see it as a toolkit for flavor. You don't need to buy 50 jars at once. In fact, the beauty of this food is that the same core spices are used across all three cultures, just in different combinations to create entirely different personalities.

An Afghani pulao is defined by sweet, fragrant spices like green cardamom and saffron. A Pakistani karahi is robust and fiery, built on black peppercorns and dried chilis. An Indian daal is earthy and bright, singing with turmeric and cumin.

This chapter is your map. We'll build your pantry in layers, starting with the "Core Four" you'll use every day, and then adding the aromatics, spices, and fresh ingredients that give these dishes their soul. We'll also cover my "healthy swaps" and the modern tools that make this all possible.

Think of this as your one-time investment in a lifetime of incredible, healthy food.

The Three-Culture Spice Box (My Masala Dabba)

In my kitchen, I keep my most-used spices in a masala dabba, a round stainless-steel tin with small bowls inside. It's my flavor palette. We'll start with the spices that belong in here, and then cover the "extras" I keep in the cupboard.

Layer 1: The "Core Four" (Buy These First)

You will use these in more than 80% of the recipes in this book. Always buy "seeds" when you can and grind them yourself in a coffee grinder—the difference in flavor is astounding.

- Cumin (Seeds & Ground): The earthy, savory backbone of everything. We use the seeds in tadkas (sizzling oil) and the ground powder in marinades and sauces.

- Coriander (Seeds & Ground): Cumin's partner. It's bright, citrusy, and floral. The crushed seeds are the secret to Chapli Kebabs.

- Turmeric (Ground): The anti-inflammatory golden spice. It brings a bright yellow color and a subtle, musky flavor. Essential for almost all daals and sabzis (vegetable dishes).

- Red Chili Powder: This is for heat. I use Kashmiri Red Chili Powder, which is key. It has a vibrant, beautiful red color but is surprisingly mild. This allows you to add color and flavor without scorching your tongue. You can always add more heat with fresh green chilies.

Layer 2: The Aromatics (The Soul of the Pantry)

These are the whole spices that build the deep, fragrant base of our rice dishes, kormas, and braises.

- Green Cardamom Pods: The "queen of spices." Intensely fragrant, sweet, and floral. This is the signature flavor of Afghani pulao and Indian kheer (rice pudding).

- Black Cardamom Pods: The "king." Smoky, dark, and menthol-cool. This is the secret to a robust Pakistani nihari or a restaurant-style Daal Makhani.

- Cinnamon (Cassia Bark): When we cook savory, we use the hard, reddish-brown bark, not the delicate "true" cinnamon. It's spicy and strong and infuses broths and rice with warmth.

- Cloves (Whole): Pungent, sweet, and medicinal. A little goes a long way, but it's essential for a good garam masala.

- Black Peppercorns (Whole): We use this for a different kind of heat than chili—a sharp, floral fire. Essential for a Peshawari Karahi.

Layer 3: The "Magic" Spices (The Finishing Touches)

These are the game-changers. They are the unique flavors that will make your food taste truly authentic.

- Kasoori Methi (Dried Fenugreek Leaves): If you've ever wondered what that "restaurant" flavor is, it's this. Crushing these dried leaves between your palms releases an incredible savory, herby, and slightly bitter aroma. We stir it into buttery curries and daals at the very end.

- Anardana (Dried Pomegranate Seeds): This is the signature of the Khyber Pass. Tart, fruity, and tangy, it adds a sourness that is completely unique. We use it (whole or ground) in chapli kebabs and chana masala.

- Amchur (Dried Mango Powder): A purely Indian souring agent. It adds a bright, zesty pucker to vegetable dishes and marinades.

- Kala Namak (Himalayan Black Salt): A volcanic rock salt with a high sulfur content, which gives it a surprisingly "eggy" and savory, funky flavor. It's the magic in our Khyber Cooler and raita.

- Saffron: The most precious spice. These fragrant red threads give a beautiful golden color and a flavor of honey and hay. A must-have for Afghani pulao and our lightened-up sweets.

My Homemade Spice Blends

Why buy a stale jar of garam masala when you can make a fresh, potent one in two minutes? A cheap coffee grinder dedicated to spices is your best friend.

Zara's "Warm" Garam Masala (Pakistani/Indian-Style)

This is your all-purpose finishing spice for curries and daals. In a spice grinder, blend: 2 tablespoons cumin seeds, 2 tablespoons coriander seeds, 1 tablespoon black peppercorns, 2-3 black cardamom pods (seeds only), 5-6 green cardamom pods, a 2-inch stick of cinnamon, and 1 teaspoon whole cloves. Store in an airtight jar.

Zara's "Fragrant" Pulao Masala (Afghani-Style)

This is the blend for our Kabuli Pulao and other delicate rice dishes. In a spice grinder, blend: 2 tablespoons coriander seeds, 2 tablespoons cumin seeds, 10-12 green cardamom pods, 1 star anise (optional), a 1-inch stick of cinnamon, and ½ teaspoon whole cloves.

The "Fresh" Essentials (My Countertop & Fridge)

- Ginger-Garlic Paste: You will use this in almost every savory recipe. You can buy it in a jar, but making it fresh is a 5-minute task that changes everything.

    - My Hack: In a blender, combine 1 cup of peeled garlic cloves and 1 cup of roughly chopped, peeled ginger with 2 tablespoons of avocado oil (which acts as a preservative). Blend to a smooth paste. Store in a jar in the fridge for up to two weeks.

- Onions: The foundation of all curries. I use red onions for their sharp, robust flavor in kebabs and salads, and yellow onions for a sweeter, milder base in kormas and daals.

- Tomatoes: I use canned crushed or puréed tomatoes for almost all my cooked sauces. They provide consistent, concentrated flavor. I save fresh, ripe tomatoes for salads (kachumber) and for topping chapli kebabs.

- Cilantro & Mint: These are not garnishes; they are ingredients. We use them by the handful. Buy them fresh, wash them, and store them wrapped in a damp paper towel in the fridge.

- Green Chilies: I use Thai bird or serrano chilies for clean, bright heat. We add them with the ginger and garlic to build a fiery base, or slit them and add them at the end for a fresh, spicy aroma.

- Lemons & Limes: For a final squeeze of acid to brighten up a heavy daal or a rich korma. Never serve a South Asian meal without a bowl of lemon wedges.

My Healthy Toolkit: The Modern Swaps

Here is how we get all the richness and comfort of the original dishes while keeping them light and nutritious.

For Creaminess (The "Makhan" Hack)

- Plain Greek Yogurt (Full-Fat): This is my number one swap. It replaces heavy cream in daals, kormas, and marinades. The key is to "temper" it (see the Daal Makhani recipe) by mixing it with a little hot sauce before adding it to the pot, so it doesn't curdle.

- Raw Cashews: When you need that pure, rich, Mughal-style luxury, you soak and blend raw cashews with water. The result is a "cashew cream" that is healthier than dairy and gives a korma an unbeatable silky body.

- Lite Coconut Milk: For our coastal Indian-inspired curries, lite coconut milk gives us all the flavor with a fraction of the saturated fat.

For Cooking (The "Oil" Hack)

A traditional recipe might call for a cup of ghee (clarified butter) or oil. We use a fraction of that, and we use it strategically.

- Avocado Oil: This is my high-heat cooking oil. It has a neutral flavor and a high smoke point, making it the perfect oil for the air fryer and for searing kebabs.

- Olive Oil or Ghee (in small amounts): I use these for flavor, not for cooking. A single teaspoon of ghee or a good olive oil, sizzled at the end with spices (a tadka), and drizzled over a daal gives you 100% of the flavor for 10% of the fat.

The Pantry Staples (The "Lentils, Grains & Binders")

- Lentils & Legumes (Dried & Canned): My pantry is never without whole black lentils (urad daal), yellow split lentils (moong or masoor), red split lentils (masoor), dried chickpeas, and canned chickpeas and kidney beans (rajma).

- Basmati Rice: This is essential. The long-grain, fragrant rice is the only choice for a perfect pulao or fluffy side.

- Oat Flour & Chickpea Flour (Besan): These are my healthy binders. Instead of using breadcrumbs or cornflour (cornstarch), I use these whole-grain, high-protein flours to hold my kebabs together and to create a crispy, gluten-free crust for pakoras.

My Healthy Toolkit: The Modern Swaps

Here is how we get all the richness and comfort of the original dishes while keeping them light and nutritious.

For Creaminess (The "Makhan" Hack)

- Plain Greek Yogurt (Full-Fat): This is my number one swap. It replaces heavy cream in daals, kormas, and marinades. The key is to "temper" it (see the Daal Makhani recipe) by mixing it with a little hot sauce before adding it to the pot, so it doesn't curdle.

- Raw Cashews: When you need that pure, rich, Mughal-style luxury, you soak and blend raw cashews with water. The result is a "cashew cream" that is healthier than dairy and gives a korma an unbeatable silky body.

- Lite Coconut Milk: For our coastal Indian-inspired curries, lite coconut milk gives us all the flavor with a fraction of the saturated fat.

For Cooking (The "Oil" Hack)

A traditional recipe might call for a cup of ghee (clarified butter) or oil. We use a fraction of that, and we use it strategically.

- Avocado Oil: This is my high-heat cooking oil. It has a neutral flavor and a high smoke point, making it the perfect oil for the air fryer and for searing kebabs.

- Olive Oil or Ghee (in small amounts): I use these for flavor, not for cooking. A single teaspoon of ghee or a good olive oil, sizzled at the end with spices (a tadka), and drizzled over a daal gives you 100% of the flavor for 10% of the fat.

The Pantry Staples (The "Lentils, Grains & Binders")

- Lentils & Legumes (Dried & Canned): My pantry is never without whole black lentils (urad daal), yellow split lentils (moong or masoor), red split lentils (masoor), dried chickpeas, and canned chickpeas and kidney beans (rajma).

- Basmati Rice: This is essential. The long-grain, fragrant rice is the only choice for a perfect pulao or fluffy side.

- Oat Flour & Chickpea Flour (Besan): These are my healthy binders. Instead of using breadcrumbs or cornflour (cornstarch), I use these whole-grain, high-protein flours to hold my kebabs together and to create a crispy, gluten-free crust for pakoras.

The Modern Workhorses (The Tools)

Finally, this book is built on three key pieces of equipment.

- The Air Fryer: This is my modern tandoor. It's not just for making "healthy" fries. It's a high-heat, convection-roasting machine. It's how we get a smoky char on our Chicken Tikka and a perfect, crispy-edged crust on our Chapli Kebabs and Pakoras—all with just a light spray of oil.

- The Slow Cooker: This is my patient degh, the traditional pot for slow-simmering. It's the secret to a Daal Makhani that tastes like it's been simmering all day (because it has, but without you). It breaks down tough cuts of lamb for Nihari until they are meltingly tender, and it does it all while you're at work.

- A Good Blender: This is my masalchi (spice grinder) and lassi-maker in one. It's essential for making a velvety-smooth korma sauce, a vibrant green chutney, or a refreshing Khyber Cooler.

CHAPTER 2

Morning Elixirs & Sunset Sharbat

In my family, a meal is never just about the food; it's about the drink that comes with it. A sharbat (from the Arabic shariba, "to drink") isn't just a beverage; it's an act of hospitality, a way to cool the body, and a boost for digestion.

We start the day with lassis and juices to awaken the system and end it with fragrant, cooling drinks to settle and refresh the palate.

This chapter is a collection of my favorite elixirs, all inspired by the three cultures. You won't find any refined sugars here. Instead, we'll use the natural sweetness of mango, pomegranate, and dates, and the powerful, fragrant spices of the Silk Road—turmeric, cardamom, saffron, and rose water.

These drinks are your daily dose of health, bottled in the vibrant colors of our heritage. They are the perfect, easy entry into The New Silk Road Kitchen.

The "Golden Glow" Mango Turmeric Lassi

This is not the heavy, syrupy mango lassi you get from a takeaway. This is your morning smoothie, reimagined. We use high-protein Greek yogurt, the natural sweetness of a ripe mango, and a powerful pinch of turmeric.

The secret ingredient? A tiny twist of black pepper. It's a traditional Ayurvedic trick: the piperine in the pepper dramatically boosts your body's ability to absorb the anti-inflammatory curcumin in the turmeric. It's a bright, energizing, and gut-healthy way to start your day.

PREP 5 MIN   **COOK 15 MIN**   **SERVES 1-2**

The "Golden Glow" Mango Turmeric Lassi

INGREDIENTS

- 1 cup ripe mango, fresh or frozen chunks
- ¾ cup plain Greek yogurt (2% or full-fat)
- ½ cup cold water (or unsweetened almond milk for extra creaminess)
- ½ teaspoon ground turmeric
- ¼ teaspoon ground cardamom
- 1 tiny pinch of freshly ground black pepper (you won't taste it!)
- 1 teaspoon honey or maple syrup (optional, only if your mango isn't sweet)
- Garnish: A few strands of saffron or chopped pistachios

Instructions:

- Blend: Add all ingredients—mango, Greek yogurt, cold water, turmeric, cardamom, and black pepper—to a high-speed blender.

- Taste: Blend on high for 45-60 seconds until perfectly smooth and creamy. Taste for sweetness; if the mango isn't sweet enough, add the optional honey and blend for another 10 seconds.

- Serve: Pour into a chilled glass. Garnish with a sprinkle of pistachios or a few strands of saffron and serve immediately.

Khyber Cucumber & Mint Cooler

This is your green juice, but with the soul of the subcontinent. It's hydrating, alkalizing, and fantastic for digestion, thanks to the ginger, mint, and roasted cumin. The pinch of kala namak (black salt) gives it a savory, replenishing kick that instantly cuts through the heat. I drink this first thing in the morning or as a sunset refresher before dinner.

 PREP 5 MIN    COOK 15 MIN    SERVES 1

Khyber Cucumber & Mint Cooler

INGREDIENTS

- 1 large cucumber, roughly chopped
- 1 large handful fresh spinach
- 1 small handful fresh mint leaves
- 1-inch piece of fresh ginger, peeled
- ½ green apple, cored (optional, for a hint of sweetness)
- 2 tablespoons fresh lemon or lime juice
- ½ cup (120ml) cold water or coconut water

For the Spice Garnish (do not skip):
- 1 pinch roasted cumin powder
- 1 pinch kala namak (Himalayan black salt)
- 1 pinch black pepper

Instructions:

- Blend: Add the cucumber, spinach, mint, ginger, green apple (if using), lemon juice, and cold water to a high-speed blender.

- Blend: Secure the lid and blend on high for 60-90 seconds, or until completely smooth.

- Strain (Optional): If you prefer a smooth juice, pour the mixture through a fine-mesh sieve into a bowl, pressing on the pulp to extract all the liquid. If you have a juicer, you can juice all ingredients (except the water) directly.

- Serve: Pour the juice into a tall glass. Sprinkle the roasted cumin, kala namak, and black pepper on top. Stir once and serve immediately.

Afghani Pomegranate & Rose Elixir

In Afghani culture, the pomegranate is a sacred symbol of abundance and fertility. This drink is the purest expression of its flavor. It's a simple, elegant, and powerful antioxidant boost that feels incredibly luxurious.

We're not making a complicated syrup; we're just juicing the fresh seeds and adding a whisper of rose water. This is what you serve to a guest you want to honor. It's also my favorite non-alcoholic "wine" to serve with a rich meal.

 **PREP 5 MIN**    **COOK 15 MIN**    **SERVES 2**

Afghani Pomegranate & Rose Elixir

INGREDIENTS

- 1 cup fresh pomegranate seeds (from 1 large pomegranate)
- 1 cup cold water
- 1 teaspoon pure rose water (a little goes a long way)
- 1 tablespoon fresh lemon juice
- Garnish: A splash of sparkling water, fresh mint leaves, and a few pomegranate seeds

Instructions:

- Blend: Add the pomegranate seeds and cold water to a blender. Pulse 4-5 times just to break the seeds and release their juice. Do not blend on high, or you will grind the bitter inner pips.

- Strain: Pour the mixture through a fine-mesh sieve into a pitcher, pressing firmly on the pulp to extract every last drop of the bright red juice. Discard the pulp.

- Finish: Stir the rose water and lemon juice into the pitcher.

- Serve: Pour into two glasses filled with ice. Top with a small splash of sparkling water for a gentle fizz, and garnish with a few fresh pomegranate seeds and a sprig of mint.

Spiced 'Shikanji'
(Digestive Cumin Lemonade)

This is the ultimate savory lemonade, sold by street vendors all over North India and Pakistan. It's a digestive miracle-worker, especially on hot days or after a heavy meal. The secret is the blend of roasted cumin, ginger, and kala namak (black salt), which transforms a simple lemonade into a complex, spicy, and deeply refreshing masala drink.

 PREP 5 MIN  COOK 15 MIN  SERVES 2

Spiced 'Shikanji'
(Digestive Cumin Lemonade)

INGREDIENTS

- 2 cups cold water
- ¼ cup fresh lemon juice (about 2 large lemons)
- 2 tablespoons honey or maple syrup (or to taste)
- 1-inch piece of fresh ginger, grated
- 1 teaspoon roasted cumin powder
- ½ teaspoon kala namak (Himalayan black salt)
- ¼ teaspoon ground black pepper
- Garnish: Fresh mint leaves and thin lemon slices

Instructions:

- Grate Ginger: Grate the ginger onto a small piece of cheesecloth or into a fine-mesh tea strainer. Squeeze the juice from the ginger pulp into a pitcher. Discard the dry pulp.

- Mix: To the pitcher, add the cold water, lemon juice, honey, roasted cumin powder, kala namak, and black pepper.

- Stir: Stir vigorously until the honey is dissolved and the spices are well-distributed.

- Serve: Pour into two tall glasses filled with ice. Garnish with mint leaves and a slice of lemon.

'Badam Doodh' (Healthy Saffron & Cardamom Almond Milk)

This is a healthy, dairy-free take on the traditional Badam Doodh (almond milk) my grandmother would make. It's a warm, comforting drink traditionally given to children for brain health and to adults for energy.

Instead of boiling dairy milk with sugar, we blend soaked almonds to create our own fresh, creamy milk, lightly sweeten it with dates, and infuse it with the royal flavors of saffron and cardamom. It's wonderful served warm before bed.

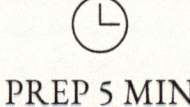 PREP 5 MIN    COOK 15 MIN    SERVES 2

'Badam Doodh' (Healthy Saffron & Cardamom Almond Milk)

INGREDIENTS

- ½ cup raw, blanched almonds, soaked overnight (or in hot water for 1 hour)
- 2 cups cold water
- 2-3 soft Medjool dates, pitted
- 1 large pinch of high-quality saffron threads
- ½ teaspoon ground cardamom
- 1 teaspoon pure rose water (optional)

Instructions:

- **Infuse:** In a small bowl, add the saffron threads to 2 tablespoons of hot (not boiling) water. Let it sit for 5 minutes to "bloom"—this will release its color and aroma.

- **Drain:** Drain the soaked almonds (their skins should slip off easily if you didn't buy blanched).

- **Blend:** Add the drained almonds, 2 cups of cold water, the pitted dates, the bloomed saffron (with its water), and the ground cardamom to a high-speed blender.

- **Blend:** Secure the lid and blend on high for 2 minutes straight. The milk should be creamy, smooth, and warm from the friction of the blender.

- **Serve:** This drink is traditionally served without straining to get all the fiber and nutrients from the almonds. Pour into two mugs and serve warm. (If you prefer a very smooth, thinner milk, you can strain it through a nut-milk bag).

Pink 'Noon' Chai (Simplified Kashmiri Chai)

This is my simplified, weeknight version of the legendary Noon Chai (Salt Tea) from Kashmir. The authentic version is a beautiful labor of love, a pink-hued, savory tea brewed for over an hour.

My "hack" uses a tiny pinch of baking soda, which reacts with the chlorophyll in the green tea to release that signature pinkish color and earthy flavor in just 15 minutes. It's savory, creamy, and fragrant with cardamom—the perfect partner for a crisp morning.

PREP 15 MIN

COOK 15 MIN

SERVES 2

Pink 'Noon' Chai
(Simplified Kashmiri Chai)

INGREDIENTS

- 2 cups cold water
- 2 teaspoons Kashmiri (or any) green tea leaves
- 3 green cardamom pods, lightly crushed
- 1 small pinch of baking soda (no more than 1/8 tsp!)
- 1 cup milk (dairy or unsweetened almond milk)
- ½ teaspoon salt (or to taste)
- Garnish: Crushed pistachios and almonds

Instructions:

- **Brew:** In a small saucepan, add the 2 cups of cold water, green tea leaves, crushed cardamom pods, and the tiny pinch of baking soda

- **Boil & Aerate:** Bring to a boil, then reduce to a rolling simmer. Let it bubble and reduce for about 10 minutes. The liquid will turn a deep, reddish-brown.

- **Strain:** Strain the tea into a separate bowl or pitcher, discarding the tea leaves.

- **Combine:** Pour the strained tea back into the saucepan. Place it over medium heat and pour in the milk.

- **Heat:** Whisk the tea and milk together and heat until it is hot, but do not let it boil.

- **Serve:** Add the salt and stir. Pour into two cups (pyalas) and garnish with a sprinkle of crushed pistachios and almonds

CHAPTER 3

The Modern Tandoor

(Air Fryer Kebabs, Tikkas & Crispy Bites)

Welcome to my favorite chapter. This is where we rewrite the rules.

In my family, the best foods were "outside" foods. They came from the fiery heat of the tandoor oven—smoky tikkas, charred kebabs—or the sizzling, bubbling kadhai (a deep-frying wok) that gave us crispy pakoras and Lahori fish. These were celebration foods, party foods, street foods. They were also, traditionally, heavy foods, drenched in oil or ghee.

For years, I tried to replicate them at home. My oven broiler was a pale imitation; it baked a kebab, it didn't char it. My attempts at "healthy" deep-frying were messy and disappointing.

Then, I discovered the air fryer. And I realized it wasn't a gimmicky gadget for french fries—it was my modern tandoor.

The air fryer is, in essence, a small, high-powered convection oven. Its contained, circulating hot air mimics the intense, all-over heat of a clay oven. It's how we get a smoky char on our Chicken Tikka. It's how we get a perfectly rendered crust on a Chapli Kebab. And it's how we achieve a shatteringly crispy Pakora with just a light spray of oil.

This chapter is your gateway to all the crispy, smoky, celebratory foods you love, made any night of the week. This is how we bring the street food and the tandoor into our healthy, modern kitchen.

Air Fryer Peshawari Chapli Kebabs

The chapli kebab is the king of kebabs, hailing from Peshawar. Traditionally, these wide, flat patties are shallow-fried in a kadhai of hot oil, resulting in a crispy crust and juicy center. My father's version is legendary, but it's a heavy affair.

Here, the air fryer works its magic. By adding a little oat flour (my healthy swap for the traditional corn or gram flour) as a binder, the lean mince stays incredibly moist while the air fryer creates that signature crust with just a light spray of oil.

PREP 15 MIN   COOK 12-14 MIN   SERVES 4

Air Fryer Peshawari Chapli Kebabs

INGREDIENTS

- 1 lb (450g) lean ground chicken, turkey, or beef (90/10)
- 1 small onion, very finely chopped
- 1 large tomato, deseeded and finely chopped (plus 1 tomato, thinly sliced for topping)
- 2-3 green chilies, finely minced
- ¼ cup fresh cilantro, finely chopped
- 1 tablespoon fresh ginger-garlic paste
- 1 egg, lightly beaten
- 2 tablespoons oat flour or chickpea flour (as a binder)
- 1 tablespoon ground coriander, coarsely crushed
- 1 teaspoon cumin seeds
- 1 teaspoon dried pomegranate seeds (anardana), lightly crushed (this is the secret!)
- 1 teaspoon red chili flakes
- 1 teaspoon kosher salt
- Avocado oil spray (or other high-heat oil)

Instructions:

- Toast Spices: In a small, dry pan over medium heat, toast the ground coriander, cumin seeds, and pomegranate seeds for 1-2 minutes until fragrant. This blooms their flavor.
- Mix Kebabs: In a large bowl, combine the ground meat, chopped onion, chopped tomato, green chilies, cilantro, ginger-garlic paste, egg, and flour. Add the toasted spices, chili flakes, and salt.
- Combine: Mix everything gently with your hands. Do not overwork the meat, or it will become tough.
- Form Patties: Wet your hands. Divide the mixture into 8 equal portions and flatten them into thin, wide patties (about ½-inch thick). Press one thin slice of tomato gently onto the top of each patty.
- Air Fry: Preheat your air fryer to 390°F (200°C). Spray the basket lightly with oil.
- Cook: Place 4 kebabs in the basket in a single layer, tomato-side-up. Spray the tops lightly with oil. Air fry for 10-14 minutes, carefully flipping them halfway through, until golden brown, crisp at the edges, and cooked through.
- Serve: Repeat with the remaining kebabs. Serve immediately with the Avocado-Mint Chutney and quick-pickled onions.

Air Fryer Tandoori Chicken Tikka

This is the one. That smoky, spicy, yogurt-marinated chicken that is the star of every South Asian restaurant. The secret to tikka is a two-part marinade and high, high heat. Greek yogurt tenderizes the chicken, and the spices create a flavorful crust.

The air fryer is the perfect tool to get the tandoori "char" (those little blackened bits) that a regular oven just can't replicate. Serve this as an appetizer, or roll it in a roti with pickled onions for a delicious, healthy wrap.

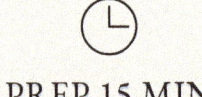 PREP 15 MIN    COOK 12-15 MIN   SERVES 4

Air Fryer Tandoori Chicken Tikka

INGREDIENTS

- 1.5 lbs (680g) boneless, skinless chicken thighs or breasts, cut into 1.5-inch chunks
- 1 tablespoon fresh lemon juice
- 1 teaspoon kosher salt
- 1 cup plain Greek yogurt (full-fat is best)
- 1.5 tablespoons ginger-garlic paste
- 2 tablespoons avocado oil (or other neutral oil)
- 1.5 teaspoons Kashmiri red chili powder (for color)
- 1 teaspoon ground cumin
- 1 teaspoon ground coriander
- ½ teaspoon garam masala
- ½ teaspoon turmeric powder
- ¼ teaspoon smoked paprika (optional, for extra smoke)
- Avocado oil spray

Instructions:

- First Marinade: In a medium bowl, toss the chicken chunks with the lemon juice and salt. Set aside for 15 minutes. This step is crucial for tenderizing.

- Second Marinade: In a separate, large bowl, whisk together the Greek yogurt, ginger-garlic paste, oil, Kashmiri chili powder, cumin, coriander, garam masala, turmeric, and smoked paprika (if using).

- Combine: Add the chicken to the yogurt marinade and mix until every piece is thoroughly coated. Cover and refrigerate for at least 1 hour, or up to 8 hours.

- Preheat: Preheat your air fryer to 400°F (200°C).

- Cook: Spray the air fryer basket with oil. Arrange the chicken pieces in a single layer, leaving a little space between them (you will need to do this in two batches). Do not overcrowd the basket.

- Air Fry: Spray the tops of the chicken with oil. Air fry for 10-15 minutes, flipping the pieces halfway through. The tikka is done when it's cooked through and has developed dark, charred spots on the edges.

- Serve: Serve hot with lemon wedges for squeezing and Cucumber & Cumin Raita.

Lahori 'Fried' Fish

The street food of Lahore is legendary, and this spicy, tangy "fried" fish is one of its most famous dishes. The authentic version is coated in a spiced chickpea-flour batter and deep-fried.

My version keeps all the flavor but skips the oil bath. The ajwain (carom seeds) are essential—they have a unique, thyme-like flavor that is the signature of this dish. A light, double-dredge in spiced chickpea flour gives us a fantastic, crispy crust in the air fryer.

 PREP 10 MIN  COOK 10-12 MIN  SERVES 4

Lahori 'Fried' Fish

INGREDIENTS

- 1.5 lbs (680g) firm white fish (like cod, haddock, or tilapia), cut into 2-inch pieces
- 1 tablespoon lemon juice
- 1 tablespoon ginger-garlic paste
- 1 teaspoon ajwain (carom seeds), lightly crushed
- 1 teaspoon Kashmiri red chili powder
- ½ teaspoon salt
- ¾ cup chickpea flour (besan)
- 1 teaspoon ground coriander
- ½ teaspoon ground cumin
- ½ teaspoon turmeric powder
- Avocado oil spray

Instructions:

- Marinate: In a bowl, gently toss the fish pieces with the lemon juice, ginger-garlic paste, ajwain, chili powder, and salt. Let it marinate for 20 minutes.

- Set Up Dredge: In a shallow dish, whisk together the chickpea flour, ground coriander, cumin, and turmeric.

- Coat: Take a piece of fish, letting any excess marinade drip off, and dredge it in the chickpea flour, pressing gently to coat all sides. Shake off the excess. Place it on a clean plate. Repeat with all the fish.

- Preheat: Preheat your air fryer to 400°F (200°C).

- Air Fry: Spray the air fryer basket with oil. Place the fish pieces in a single layer, not touching. Spray the tops of the fish generously with oil (this is key to getting the flour crispy).

- Cook: Air fry for 10-12 minutes, carefully flipping halfway through and spraying the other side with oil. The fish is done when the crust is golden and crisp and the fish flakes easily.

- Serve: Serve immediately, sprinkled with chaat masala (a tangy spice blend) and a side of Avocado-Mint Chutney.

Crispy Onion & Spinach Pakoras

The ultimate rainy-day snack. Pakoras (or bhajis) are spiced vegetable fritters. The problem? They are delicious, but they are also oil-sponges.

After many (many!) failed attempts, I cracked the code for a light, crispy air fryer pakora. The secret is to use very little water. You want a thick, sticky batter that just barely holds the vegetables together. The moisture from the onions and spinach is all you need. This makes them light and crispy, not dense and cakey.

 PREP 10 MIN   COOK 12-14 MIN   SERVES 4

Crispy Onion & Spinach Pakoras

INGREDIENTS

- 1 large onion, thinly sliced
- 2 cups packed fresh spinach, roughly chopped
- 1 green chili, finely minced
- 1 teaspoon grated fresh ginger
- 1 cup chickpea flour (besan)
- 1 teaspoon ground coriander
- 1 teaspoon ground cumin
- ½ teaspoon red chili powder
- ½ teaspoon turmeric powder
- ½ teaspoon ajwain (carom seeds)
- ¾ teaspoon kosher salt
- 2-3 tablespoons cold water (and no more!)
- Avocado oil spray

Instructions:

- **Mix Veg:** In a large bowl, combine the sliced onion, chopped spinach, green chili, and ginger. Sprinkle with the salt and use your hands to massage the vegetables for about 30 seconds. This will help them release their natural moisture.

- **Add Spices & Flour:** Add the chickpea flour, coriander, cumin, chili powder, turmeric, and ajwain. Toss to coat the vegetables in the dry flour.

- **Form Batter:** Add 2 tablespoons of water and mix with your hands until a thick, sticky batter forms. It should not be runny! If it's still too dry and powdery, add the last tablespoon of water. You want a paste, not a batter. Let it sit for 5 minutes.

- **Preheat:** Preheat your air fryer to 380°F (190°C). Spray the basket generously with oil.

- **Cook:** Drop heaping tablespoons of the batter into the basket, leaving space between them. Spray the tops of the pakoras very generously with oil.

- **Air Fry:** Cook for 12-14 minutes, flipping them halfway through and spraying the other side with oil. They are done when they are deep golden brown and feel dry and crispy to the touch.

- **Serve:** Serve immediately with Date & Tamarind Chutney.

Banjan Borani
(Afghani Silky Eggplant with Yogurt)

This dish is, in my opinion, one of the most delicious ways to eat eggplant on earth. It's a classic meze from Afghanistan. Traditionally, thick slices of eggplant are fried in a lot of oil until silky, then layered with a bright tomato sauce and a cool, garlicky yogurt (chakkah).

The air fryer is a complete game-changer here. We can achieve that same meltingly tender, silky texture with a fraction of the oil, turning a heavy indulgence into a healthy, elegant vegetable side.

PREP 10 MIN **COOK 20 MIN** **SERVES 4**

Banjan Borani
(Afghani Silky Eggplant with Yogurt)

INGREDIENTS

- 1 large globe eggplant, cut into ½-inch thick rounds
- 2-3 tablespoons olive or avocado oil
- 1 teaspoon kosher salt
- 1 cup plain Greek yogurt
- 1 clove garlic, minced or grated
- 1 tablespoon olive oil
- 1 onion, finely chopped
- 2 cloves garlic, thinly sliced
- 1 (15oz) can crushed tomatoes
- ½ teaspoon turmeric powder
- Salt and pepper to taste
- Garnish: Dried mint and fresh cilantro

Instructions:

- Cook Eggplant: Preheat your air fryer to 400°F (200°C). In a large bowl, toss the eggplant rounds with the 2-3 tablespoons of oil and salt.

- Air Fry: Place the eggplant in a single layer in the air fryer (work in batches). Cook for 15-20 minutes, flipping halfway, until the eggplant is deep brown, caramelized, and very tender.

- Make Yogurt: While the eggplant cooks, mix the Greek yogurt with the 1 minced garlic clove and a pinch of salt. Spread this in a thin layer on the bottom of your serving platter.

- Make Sauce: In a skillet over medium heat, heat the 1 tablespoon of olive oil. Add the onion and cook until soft (5-7 minutes). Add the sliced garlic and cook for 1 more minute until fragrant.

- Simmer: Add the crushed tomatoes, turmeric, salt, and pepper. Bring to a simmer and cook for 10-15 minutes until the sauce has thickened.

- Assemble: Arrange the cooked, hot eggplant slices on top of the yogurt layer. Spoon the warm tomato sauce over the eggplant.

- Garnish: Drizzle with a little extra yogurt, sprinkle with dried mint and fresh cilantro, and serve.

Tandoori-Style Paneer & Pepper Skewers

This is the vegetarian answer to Chicken Tikka and just as good. Paneer is a firm, non-melting Indian cottage cheese. Its mild, milky flavor is the perfect canvas for a spicy tandoori marinade.

The key is to cut the paneer and vegetables into large, 1-inch chunks so they don't overcook. The air fryer chars the edges of the peppers and onions while keeping the paneer soft and squeaky in the center.

 PREP 15 MIN   COOK 10-12 MIN   SERVES 2-3

Tandoori-Style Paneer & Pepper Skewers

INGREDIENTS

- 8 oz (225g) block of paneer, cut into 1-inch cubes
- 1 large green bell pepper, cut into 1-inch chunks
- 1 large red onion, cut into 1-inch chunks
- ½ cup plain Greek yogurt
- 1 tablespoon ginger-garlic paste
- 1 tablespoon lemon juice
- 1 tablespoon avocado oil
- 1.5 teaspoons Kashmiri red chili powder
- 1 teaspoon ground coriander
- 1 teaspoon ground cumin
- ½ teaspoon garam masala
- ½ teaspoon turmeric powder
- ½ teaspoon ajwain (carom seeds)
- ½ teaspoon kosher salt
- Avocado oil spray
- Optional: 4-6 wooden skewers, soaked in water for 30 minutes

Instructions:

- Marinate: In a large bowl, whisk together the Greek yogurt, ginger-garlic paste, lemon juice, oil, and all the spices.

- Combine: Gently add the paneer, bell pepper, and onion to the bowl. Use your hands to carefully coat everything in the marinade (be gentle with the paneer!). Let it marinate for at least 30 minutes.

- Preheat: Preheat your air fryer to 390°F (200°C).

- Assemble: Thread the marinated paneer, onion, and pepper chunks onto the soaked wooden skewers, alternating them. (Or, you can just place the loose chunks directly in the basket, which is even faster!).

- Air Fry: Spray the basket with oil. Place the skewers (or loose chunks) in a single layer. Spray the tops with oil.

- Cook: Air fry for 10-12 minutes, flipping halfway through, until the paneer is lightly browned and the vegetables are soft and charred at the edges.

- Serve: Serve hot, sprinkled with chaat masala and a squeeze of fresh lemon.

Spiced Cauliflower 'Steaks' with Mint Chutney

This is my modern, plant-based take on a tandoori main. By cutting a head of cauliflower into thick "steaks," we create a hearty, satisfying dish. The spice-infused yogurt marinade forms a delicious crust in the air fryer. This is a fantastic, light dinner or an impressive side dish.

PREP 10 MIN   COOK 15-18 MIN   SERVES 2

Spiced Cauliflower 'Steaks' with Mint Chutney

INGREDIENTS

- 1 large head of cauliflower
- ½ cup plain Greek yogurt
- 1 tablespoon ginger-garlic paste
- 1 tablespoon avocado oil
- 1 tablespoon lemon juice
- 1 teaspoon ground cumin
- 1 teaspoon ground coriander
- 1 teaspoon smoked paprika
- ½ teaspoon turmeric powder
- ½ teaspoon kosher salt
- Avocado oil spray
- For Serving: Avocado-Mint Chutney and pomegranate seeds

Instructions:

- Cut Steaks: Trim the leaves and bottom stem of the cauliflower. Stand it upright and carefully cut two or three 1-inch thick "steaks" from the center. (The side florets will crumble; save them for Aloo Gobi!).

- Make Marinade: In a small bowl, whisk together the Greek yogurt, ginger-garlic paste, oil, lemon juice, and all the spices.

- Coat: Place the cauliflower steaks on a baking sheet. Brush the marinade generously on all sides, getting it into the crevices.

- Preheat: Preheat your air fryer to 380°F (190°C).

- Air Fry: Spray the basket with oil. Carefully place the steaks in the basket (you may need to do this one at a time if they are large). Spray the tops with oil.

- Cook: Air fry for 15-18 minutes, gently flipping about 10 minutes in. The steaks are done when they are tender all the way through and deeply browned and caramelized on the outside.

- Serve: Serve the cauliflower steak hot, drizzled with the Avocado-Mint Chutney and a sprinkle of fresh pomegranate seeds.

Afghani 'Bolani'
(Crispy Stuffed Flatbread)

Bolani is a beloved Afghani street food, a thin flatbread stuffed with a savory filling, traditionally pan-fried until blistered and crisp. The most common fillings are potato (kachaloo), leek (gandana), or lentil.

Here, we use a simple store-bought raw flour tortilla as a "hack" for the dough, which saves hours of work. The air fryer gets the bolani incredibly crispy and golden with just a brush of oil. It's the perfect appetizer or light lunch, served with a cooling yogurt dip.

 PREP 20 MIN   COOK 10-12 MIN   SERVES 4

Afghani 'Bolani' (Crispy Stuffed Flatbread)

INGREDIENTS

- 1 large potato (about 1.5 cups), peeled and boiled
- 1 green onion, finely chopped
- 2 tablespoons fresh cilantro, finely chopped
- 1 green chili, finely minced (optional)
- 1 teaspoon ground coriander
- Salt and black pepper to taste
- 4-6 large, raw flour tortillas (the un-cooked kind found in the refrigerated section)
- Olive or avocado oil, for brushing
- **For Serving:**
- Chakkah (Garlicky Yogurt) or plain Greek yogurt

Instructions:

- Make Filling: In a medium bowl, mash the boiled potato. Add the green onion, cilantro, green chili (if using), coriander, salt, and pepper. Mix well to combine.

- Assemble: Lay a raw tortilla on your work surface. Spread about ½ cup of the potato filling evenly over one half of the tortilla.

- Fold: Fold the empty half of the tortilla over the filling to create a half-moon shape. Press down firmly, sealing the edges.

- Preheat: Preheat your air fryer to 380°F (190°C).

- Cook: Brush both sides of the bolani lightly with oil. Place it in the air fryer basket (you will have to do this one at a time).

- Air Fry: Cook for 10-12 minutes, flipping halfway through. The bolani is done when it is golden brown, puffed up in spots, and crispy.

- Serve: Cut the hot bolani into wedges and serve immediately with the garlicky yogurt for dipping.

CHAPTER 4

The Patient Pot

(Soulful Kormas, Curries & Daals from the Slow Cooker)

If the last chapter was about speed and high heat, this one is about the magic of its opposite: patience.

This chapter is my ode to the degh, the traditional, heavy-bottomed pot used for dum pukht, or the art of slow-cooking. This is how you build deep, complex, and meltingly tender flavors—the kind that taste like a grandmother spent her entire day tending the stove.

But we have lives. We have jobs. We have things to do. We don't have eight hours to stir a pot.

This is where the slow cooker becomes our most trusted ally. It is our modern, electric degh. It's how we achieve that all-day-simmered Nihari... while we're at work. It's how a Daal Makhani can simmer safely overnight, breaking down into a creamy, luxurious stew by itself, without a single pat of butter or drop of cream.

These are the "set it and forget it" recipes that form the soulful, comforting heart of the New Silk Road. This is how we make time our servant, not our master.

'Zero-Ghee' Slow Cooker Daal Makhani

This is the ultimate "set it and forget it" recipe for the most luxurious daal on earth. Traditionally, Daal Makhani (which means "Buttery Lentils") is loaded with butter and heavy cream and simmered for hours.

My version builds its own creaminess from the slow-cooking process, which breaks down the lentils perfectly. The "secret" is to finish it with a swirl of Greek yogurt instead of cream and a tiny, 1-teaspoon tadka (tempered spice) of smoked paprika, which mimics the smoky flavor of a tandoor without any of the fat.

 PREP 10 MIN   **COOK 8-10 HOURS**   **SERVES 6**

'Zero-Ghee' Slow Cooker Daal Makhani

INGREDIENTS

For the Slow Cooker (Phase 1):
- 1 cup whole black lentils (urad daal), rinsed and soaked overnight
- ¼ cup red kidney beans (rajma), rinsed and soaked overnight
- 1 large onion, finely chopped
- 2-inch piece of ginger, peeled and grated
- 4 cloves garlic, grated
- 1 green chili, slit lengthwise
- 1 teaspoon kosher salt
- 4 cups water

For Finishing (The Healthy 'Makhan'):
- ½ cup plain Greek yogurt (full-fat recommended)
- 1 teaspoon avocado or olive oil
- ½ teaspoon smoked paprika (this is the smoky flavor hack!)
- 1 teaspoon kasoori methi (dried fenugreek leaves)
- Fresh cilantro, for garnish

For the Masala (Phase 2):
- 1 (15oz) can crushed tomatoes (or 4 fresh tomatoes, puréed)
- 1 teaspoon Kashmiri red chili powder (for color)
- 1 teaspoon garam masala
- ½ teaspoon ground coriander
- ½ teaspoon ground cumin

Instructions:

- Phase 1 (Overnight): Drain the soaked lentils and kidney beans. Add them to the bowl of a 6-quart slow cooker. Add the chopped onion, ginger, garlic, green chili, salt, and 4 cups of water. Stir to combine.

- Cook: Cover and cook on LOW for 8-10 hours or on HIGH for 5-6 hours. The lentils and beans should be completely tender and breaking apart.

- Phase 2 (The Masala): Do not drain. Stir the crushed tomatoes, Kashmiri chili powder, garam masala, coriander, and cumin directly into the slow cooker.

- Simmer: Cover and cook on HIGH for 1 more hour to let the flavors marry and the sauce thicken.

- Finish: Just before serving, prepare the "tadka." In a tiny skillet, heat the 1 teaspoon of oil over medium heat. Add the smoked paprika and sizzle for just 10 seconds (don't let it burn). Pour this sizzling oil into the daal and stir.

- Temper Yogurt: In a small bowl, add the Greek yogurt. Add a few tablespoons of the hot daal to the yogurt and mix quickly (this is "tempering," so the yogurt doesn't curdle).

- Serve: Turn off the slow cooker. Stir in the tempered yogurt and the kasoori methi (crushing it between your palms as you add it). Garnish generously with fresh cilantro and serve hot.

Slow Cooker Lamb Shank Nihari

Nihari is a legendary, soulful stew from Old Delhi and Lahore, traditionally slow-cooked all night and eaten for breakfast. It's rich, spicy, and medicinal, with a silky gravy thickened with flour. The slow cooker is its modern soulmate.

We make a quick masala base, then let the lamb shanks simmer for 8 hours until they are so tender they fall from the bone. The final step of thickening it with a whole-wheat flour slurry is what makes it a true Nihari.

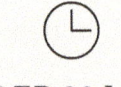 PREP 20 MIN   COOK 8 HOURS   SERVES 4

Slow Cooker Lamb Shank Nihari

INGREDIENTS

- 4 lamb shanks (about 3-4 lbs total)
- 1 tablespoon avocado oil
- 2 large onions, thinly sliced
- 2 tablespoons ginger-garlic paste
- 1 cup plain Greek yogurt
- 4 cups beef or chicken broth, low sodium
- 1 tablespoon whole-wheat flour (atta)

Nihari Spices:
- 1 tablespoon fennel seeds
- 1 teaspoon black peppercorns
- 2 black cardamom pods
- 1-inch stick of cinnamon
- 4-5 cloves
- 1 tablespoon Kashmiri red chili powder
- 1 teaspoon ground ginger
- 1 teaspoon turmeric powder

For Garnish (Essential!):
- 1-inch piece of ginger, cut into thin matchsticks
- 2-3 green chilies, thinly sliced
- Fresh cilantro
- Lemon wedges

Instructions:

- Make Masala: In a spice grinder, toast and grind the fennel seeds, peppercorns, black cardamom, cinnamon, and cloves. Transfer to a small bowl and mix with the chili powder, ground ginger, and turmeric.

- Sauté Base: In a large skillet over medium-high heat, heat the oil. Add the onions and cook for 8-10 minutes until golden. Add the ginger-garlic paste and the spice blend and cook for 1-2 minutes until fragrant.

- Deglaze: Add the Greek yogurt and 1 cup of the broth, stirring and scraping the bottom of the pan to get all the flavorful bits.

- To the Pot: Place the lamb shanks in the slow cooker. Pour the onion-spice mixture from the skillet over the shanks. Add the remaining 3 cups of broth.

- Cook: Cover and cook on LOW for 8 hours. The meat should be completely tender.

- Thicken: Carefully remove the lamb shanks to a plate. In a small bowl, whisk the whole-wheat flour with ¼ cup of cold water to make a smooth slurry. Pour this into the slow cooker and whisk it into the gravy. Turn the slow cooker to HIGH and cook, uncovered, for 15-20 minutes to thicken.

- Serve: Return the lamb shanks to the pot. Serve the Nihari in bowls, topped generously with the ginger matchsticks, green chilies, cilantro, and a big squeeze of lemon.

Afghani Chicken & Apricot Korma

This is an authentic Afghani Korma—and it may be different from what you expect. It isn't bright red or fiery. It's a pale, elegant, and fragrant stew, sweet with onions and apricots, and creamy from our healthy "cashew cream" hack.

The secret is to cook the onions until they are soft and translucent, not brown. This creates a sweet, pale gravy that is the hallmark of this royal dish.

 PREP 20 MIN   COOK 4-56 HOURS   SERVES 4-6

Afghani Chicken & Apricot Korma

INGREDIENTS

- 2 lbs boneless, skinless chicken thighs
- 1 tablespoon avocado oil
- 2 large yellow onions, finely chopped
- 2 tablespoons ginger-garlic paste
- 1 teaspoon ground coriander
- 1 teaspoon ground cumin
- ½ teaspoon ground white pepper (key for a pale korma)
- 1 teaspoon kosher salt
- 6-8 green cardamom pods, lightly crushed
- 1.5 cups low-sodium chicken broth
- ½ cup dried apricots, halved
- For the Creamy Finish:
- ½ cup raw, unsalted cashews, soaked
- ½ cup plain Greek yogurt
- 1 teaspoon rose water (optional)

Instructions:

- Sauté Base: In a large skillet over medium heat, heat the oil. Add the onions and a pinch of salt. Cook gently for 10-12 minutes, stirring often, until the onions are very soft and translucent, but not browned.

- Add Aromatics: Add the ginger-garlic paste, ground coriander, cumin, white pepper, and crushed cardamom. Cook for 1-2 minutes until fragrant.

- To the Pot: Transfer the onion mixture to your slow cooker. Add the chicken thighs, chicken broth, and dried apricots. Stir to combine.

- Cook: Cover and cook on LOW for 4-5 hours (or HIGH for 2.5-3 hours), until the chicken is tender.

- Make Cream: Drain the soaked cashews. In a blender, combine the cashews and Greek yogurt. Blend on high until perfectly smooth and creamy.

- Finish: Stir the cashew-yogurt cream into the slow cooker. Add the optional rose water. Let it heat through for another 10 minutes.

- Serve: Serve hot, garnished with toasted almonds and fresh cilantro.

Slow Cooker Lahori Chana Masala

The secret to a deep, dark, complex chana masala (like you get in Lahore or Amritsar) is cooking dried chickpeas from scratch with a tea bag. The tannins in the tea give the chickpeas a rich, dark color and a wonderfully complex flavor. The slow cooker makes this foolproof.

 PREP 10 MIN    COOK 8-10 HOURS    SERVES 6

Slow Cooker Lahori Chana Masala

INGREDIENTS

- 1.5 cups dried chickpeas, rinsed and soaked overnight
- 1 tablespoon avocado oil
- 1 large onion, finely chopped
- 1 tablespoon ginger-garlic paste
- 1 (15oz) can crushed tomatoes
- 2 black tea bags (any plain black tea, like English Breakfast)
- 2 black cardamom pods
- 1-inch stick of cinnamon
- 1 teaspoon ground coriander
- 1 teaspoon ground cumin
- 1 teaspoon Kashmiri red chili powder
- ½ teaspoon turmeric powder
- 4 cups water

For Finishing:

- 1 teaspoon anardana powder (dried pomegranate) OR amchur (mango powder)
- 1 teaspoon garam masala
- Fresh cilantro

Instructions:

- Sauté Base: In a skillet over medium heat, heat the oil. Sauté the onion for 5-7 minutes until soft. Add the ginger-garlic paste and cook for 1 minute. Add the crushed tomatoes and all the ground spices (coriander, cumin, chili, turmeric) and cook for 3-4 minutes.

- To the Pot: Drain the soaked chickpeas. Add them to the slow cooker. Pour the onion-tomato masala on top.

- Add Aromatics: Add the 2 black tea bags, black cardamom pods, cinnamon stick, and 4 cups of water. Stir to combine.

- Cook: Cover and cook on LOW for 8-10 hours or HIGH for 6-7 hours, until the chickpeas are very tender.

- Finish: Remove and discard the tea bags and whole spices.

- Thicken: Use an immersion blender (or a potato masher) and pulse a few times to roughly mash about ¼ of the chickpeas. This thickens the gravy beautifully.

- Serve: Stir in the anardana (or amchur) powder and the garam masala. Serve hot, topped with fresh cilantro.

Hearty Rajma
(Indian Kidney Bean Curry)

Rajma-Chawal (kidney beans with rice) is the ultimate North Indian comfort food. It's the Sunday-lunch-at-home meal, and it's pure, soulful, vegetarian protein. Using canned beans is fine for a quick version (see Chapter 5), but cooking from dried in the slow cooker creates a much creamier, more flavorful sauce that is truly next-level.

 PREP 10 MIN   COOK 8-10 Hours   SERVES 4

Hearty Rajma (Indian Kidney Bean Curry)

INGREDIENTS

- 1.5 cups dried red kidney beans, rinsed and soaked overnight
- 1 tablespoon avocado oil
- 1 large red onion, finely chopped
- 2 tablespoons ginger-garlic paste
- 1 (15oz) can crushed tomatoes
- 1 green chili, slit
- 1.5 teaspoons ground coriander
- 1 teaspoon ground cumin
- 1 teaspoon Kashmiri red chili powder
- ½ teaspoon turmeric powder
- 1 teaspoon kosher salt
- 4 cups water

For Finishing:

- 1 teaspoon garam masala
- ½ cup fresh cilantro, chopped

Instructions:

- **Sauté Base:** In a skillet over medium heat, heat the oil. Sauté the onion for 5-7 minutes until soft. Add the ginger-garlic paste and cook for 1 minute until fragrant.

- **Add Tomatoes & Spices:** Add the crushed tomatoes, green chili, and all the ground spices (coriander, cumin, chili, turmeric) and salt. Cook for 5 minutes, stirring, until the masala is thick and dark.

- **To the Pot:** Drain the soaked kidney beans. Add them to the slow cooker. Pour the masala from the skillet on top. Add the 4 cups of water and stir.

- **Cook:** Cover and cook on LOW for 8-10 hours or HIGH for 6-7 hours, until the beans are meltingly tender.

- **Thicken & Finish:** Just like the chana, use a potato masher or immersion blender to lightly mash some of the beans to create a creamy gravy.

- **Serve:** Stir in the garam masala and the fresh cilantro. Serve hot over a bed of fluffy basmati rice.

Simplified Chicken Haleem

Haleem is a celebratory dish, a thick, savory porridge of lentils, grains, and meat, slow-cooked until it's one harmonious, creamy stew. It's usually an all-day, high-labor affair involving stirring and pounding. The slow cooker, however, is a miracle here. It does all the work of breaking down the grains and chicken for you.

PREP 15MIN

COOK 8 HOURS

SERVES 6-8

Simplified Chicken Haleem

INGREDIENTS

- 1.5 lbs boneless, skinless chicken breast or thighs
- ½ cup cracked wheat or barley, rinsed and soaked for 1 hour
- ½ cup chana daal (split chickpeas), rinsed and soaked for 1 hour
- ¼ cup masoor daal (red split lentils), rinsed
- ¼ cup moong daal (yellow split lentils), rinsed
- 1 large onion, chopped
- 1 tablespoon ginger-garlic paste
- 1 teaspoon turmeric powder
- 1 teaspoon red chili powder
- 1 teaspoon ground coriander
- 1 teaspoon garam masala
- 1 teaspoon kosher salt
- 6 cups low-sodium chicken broth

For the Finishing Tadka:

- 1 tablespoon avocado oil
- 1 onion, thinly sliced
- 1 teaspoon garam masala
- Garnishes: Fried onions, fresh mint, cilantro, lemon wedges, ginger matchsticks.

Instructions:

- To the Pot: Add everything from the main ingredient list to the slow cooker: chicken, soaked grains, all the lentils, chopped onion, ginger-garlic paste, all the spices, salt, and broth.

- Cook: Stir well. Cover and cook on LOW for 8 hours.

- Shred & Blend: After 8 hours, the mixture will be thick and the chicken cooked. Remove the chicken pieces to a bowl. Shred them with two forks, then return the shredded chicken to the pot.

- Create Texture: Use an immersion blender to pulse the haleem just a few times (4-5 pulses). You are not making a smooth purée; you are just breaking down the grains to create that classic, thick, porridge-like texture.

- Make Tadka: In a skillet, heat the oil. Add the thinly sliced onion and fry until golden and crispy. Remove half the onions for garnish. To the remaining onions in the pan, add the 1 teaspoon of garam masala and sizzle for 10 seconds.

- Serve: Pour the sizzling tadka (oil, onions, and spice) over the haleem and stir it in. Serve in bowls, topped with the reserved fried onions, fresh mint, cilantro, ginger, and a squeeze of lemon.

CHAPTER 5

The Radiant Stovetop

(Quick Sabzi, Plant-Based Mains & Weeknight Grains)

While the air fryer gives us crunch and the slow cooker gives us comfort, the stovetop is where the fast, fresh, everyday magic happens. This is the domain of the kadhai and the tawa, the workhorse pans that build a healthy meal in under 30 minutes.

This chapter is the heart of my weeknight kitchen. It's where we create the vibrant sabzis (vegetable dishes) and quick daals (lentils) that form the backbone of a truly nourishing meal. In the West, these are often "side dishes," but in our homes, they are the stars.

The recipes here are naturally healthy, plant-forward, and incredibly quick. You'll learn the secret to a non-mushy Aloo Gobi. You'll master the tadka, the sizzling spice-infused oil that transforms a simple lentil soup into a masterpiece. You'll learn to make a light, bright Palak Paneer that isn't drowning in cream.

This is the food that fuels our busiest days. It's the answer to "what's for dinner?" It's fast, it's radiant, and it's the key to building a balanced, healthy plate.

Tadka Daal
(20-Minute Yellow Lentil Soup)

This is the little black dress of the South Asian kitchen. It's the 20-minute, "I-have-nothing-in-the-house" meal that is both profoundly comforting and incredibly healthy. The "magic" is the tadka (or tarka), a final tempering of spices sizzled in hot oil and poured over the cooked lentils at the very end. This floods the daal with fresh, aromatic flavor.

PREP 5 MIN

COOK 20 MIN

SERVES 4

Tadka Daal (20-Minute Yellow Lentil Soup)

INGREDIENTS

- 1 cup masoor daal (red split lentils) or moong daal (yellow split lentils), rinsed
- 3 cups water
- ½ teaspoon turmeric powder
- 1 small tomato, chopped
- 1 green chili, slit
- 1 teaspoon kosher salt (or to taste)

For the Tadka:

- 1 tablespoon avocado oil or ghee
- 1 teaspoon cumin seeds
- ½ teaspoon mustard seeds (optional)
- 1-2 dried red chilies
- 2 cloves garlic, thinly sliced
- 1 pinch of asafoetida (hing) (optional, but amazing for digestion)

Instructions:

- Cook Daal: In a medium saucepan, combine the rinsed lentils, water, turmeric, chopped tomato, green chili, and salt. Bring to a boil.

- Simmer: Reduce the heat to a simmer, partially cover, and cook for 15-20 minutes. The lentils should be very soft and broken down, forming a thick, soupy porridge.

- Make Tadka: Just before serving, prepare the tadka. In a tiny, separate skillet, heat the oil or ghee over medium-high heat. When it's hot (it should shimmer), add the cumin seeds and mustard seeds.

- Sizzle: Let the seeds "pop" and dance for about 30 seconds, then add the dried red chilies, sliced garlic, and asafoetida (if using). Swirl the pan for another 30-45 seconds, until the garlic is fragrant and golden brown (do not let it burn!).

- Bloom & Pour: Turn off the heat. You can add a pinch of Kashmiri red chili powder to the oil (off the heat) for color.

- Serve: Immediately and carefully pour the entire contents of the sizzling tadka into the pot of cooked lentils. It will sputter and steam—this is what you want! Stir once, cover for 1 minute to infuse the flavors, then serve hot, garnished with cilantro.

Restaurant-Style Aloo Gobi (Without the Mush)

Aloo Gobi (potato and cauliflower) is a beloved classic, but it has a fatal flaw: it's almost always a sad, mushy pile. The secret to a perfect, vibrant Aloo Gobi is to not add water. We let the vegetables steam in their own moisture, creating a dish that is "dry" (in a good way), where each floret is tender but still holds its shape.

PREP 10 MIN | COOK 25 MIN | SERVES 4

Restaurant-Style Aloo Gobi (Without the Mush)

INGREDIENTS

- 1 medium head of cauliflower, cut into medium florets
- 2 medium potatoes, peeled and cut into ½-inch cubes
- 1 tablespoon avocado oil
- 1 teaspoon cumin seeds
- 1 large onion, finely chopped
- 1.5 tablespoons ginger-garlic paste
- 1 large tomato, finely chopped
- 1 teaspoon ground coriander
- 1 teaspoon ground cumin
- ½ teaspoon turmeric powder
- ½ teaspoon Kashmiri red chili powder
- 1 teaspoon kosher salt
- Fresh cilantro, for garnish

Instructions:

- **Sauté Base:** In a large skillet or kadhai with a tight-fitting lid, heat the oil over medium-high heat. Add the cumin seeds and let them toast for 30 seconds.

- **Cook Onions:** Add the onion and sauté for 5-7 minutes, until softened and lightly browned. Add the ginger-garlic paste and cook for 1 minute more until fragrant.

- **Make Masala:** Add the chopped tomato and all the spices (coriander, cumin, turmeric, chili powder) and salt. Cook, stirring, for 3-4 minutes, until the tomato breaks down and the oil begins to separate from the masala.

- **Add Potatoes:** Add the cubed potatoes to the pan. Stir to coat them in the masala. Cover the pan, turn the heat to medium-low, and let the potatoes cook for 7-8 minutes.

- **Add Cauliflower:** Add the cauliflower florets to the pan. Gently stir to coat them, trying not to break them.

- **The Secret Step:** Place the lid back on, keep the heat on medium-low, and let the vegetables cook for 10-15 minutes. Do not stir! This allows the cauliflower to steam in its own moisture and the bottom to get lightly caramelized.

- **Serve:** Check for doneness. The potato and cauliflower should be tender. Gently stir once, garnish with fresh cilantro, and serve.

Bhindi Masala (Quick Okra Stir-Fry)

I'm here to solve the okra problem: slime. Okra is delicious, but when cooked incorrectly, it can have a gooey texture. The solution is simple and twofold: 1) Pat the okra completely dry after washing, and 2) Pan-fry the okra separately first, before adding it to the onion-tomato masala. This sears the outside and gives you a perfect, non-slimy bhindi every time.

PREP 15 MIN   COOK 20 MIN   SERVES 4

Bhindi Masala (Quick Okra Stir-Fry)

INGREDIENTS

- 1 lb (450g) fresh okra (bhindi), washed and thoroughly dried
- 2 tablespoons avocado oil, divided
- 1 large onion, thinly sliced
- 1 tablespoon ginger-garlic paste
- 2 medium tomatoes, chopped
- 1 teaspoon ground coriander
- ½ teaspoon ground cumin
- ½ teaspoon turmeric powder
- 1 teaspoon amchur (dried mango powder) – this is the secret!
- 1 teaspoon kosher salt
- ½ teaspoon garam masala

Instructions:

- **Prep Okra:** Trim the tops and tails from the okra. Cut them into 1-inch pieces.

- **Sear Okra:** In a large non-stick skillet, heat 1 tablespoon of the oil over medium-high heat. Add the okra in a single layer (work in batches if needed). Let it cook, undisturbed, for 3-4 minutes to get a good sear. Stir and cook for another 4-5 minutes until the okra is bright green, lightly browned, and the "slime" has cooked off. Transfer the cooked okra to a clean bowl.

- **Make Masala:** In the same skillet, add the remaining 1 tablespoon of oil. Add the sliced onion and cook for 8-10 minutes, until softened and golden brown.

- **Add Aromatics:** Add the ginger-garlic paste and cook for 1 minute. Add the chopped tomatoes, ground coriander, cumin, turmeric, and salt. Cook for 5-7 minutes, until the tomatoes have completely broken down into a thick paste.

- **Combine:** Return the cooked okra to the pan. Stir gently to coat it in the masala.

- **Serve:** Turn off the heat. Stir in the amchur (for tang) and the garam masala (for warmth). Serve immediately.

LIGHT & QUICK PALAK PANEER

This is the healthy Palak Paneer you've been searching for. So many restaurant versions are just a paneer curry with a little spinach, heavy on the cream. This recipe puts the palak (spinach) front and center. We blanch the spinach to keep its vibrant green color, and we get our creaminess from our Greek yogurt and cashew hack, not heavy cream.

PREP 10 MIN

COOK 20 MIN

SERVES 4

Light & Quick Palak Paneer

INGREDIENTS

- 10 oz (300g) fresh spinach
- 1 (8oz) block of paneer, cut into 1-inch cubes
- 1 tablespoon avocado oil
- 1 teaspoon cumin seeds
- 1 medium onion, finely chopped
- 1 tablespoon ginger-garlic paste
- 1 tomato, finely chopped
- 1 teaspoon ground coriander
- ½ teaspoon Kashmiri red chili powder
- ½ teaspoon kosher salt
- ¼ cup plain Greek yogurt OR 2 tablespoons cashew cream (see note)
- ½ teaspoon garam masala

Instructions:

- Blanch Spinach: Bring a pot of water to a boil. Add the fresh spinach and push it down. Cook for only 60 seconds. Drain immediately and rinse under ice-cold water (this is called "shocking" and it locks in the bright green color). Squeeze out all excess water and blend the spinach in a blender until smooth. Set aside.

- Sear Paneer: In a large skillet, heat ½ tablespoon of the oil. Add the paneer cubes and pan-fry for a few minutes per side until golden. (Or, air fry them for 8 minutes at 400°F!). Remove and set aside.

- Make Masala: In the same skillet, add the remaining oil and the cumin seeds. When they sizzle, add the onion and cook for 5-7 minutes until soft. Add the ginger-garlic paste and cook for 1 minute.

- Add Tomato: Add the tomato, ground coriander, chili powder, and salt. Cook for 5 minutes, until the tomato is soft.

- Combine: Stir in the spinach purée. Let it bubble and cook for 3-4 minutes.

- Finish: Turn the heat to low. Stir in the Greek yogurt or cashew cream. Add the seared paneer cubes. Stir gently to combine.

- Serve: Sprinkle with the garam masala and serve hot.

THE PERFECT, FLUFFY BASMATI RICE

A non-negotiable. Perfect, separate, fluffy grains of basmati rice are the foundation of a good meal. People are often intimidated by it, but the method is simple and foolproof. The three secrets are: Rinse, Soak, and Don't Peek.

 PREP 5 MIN    COOK 20 MIN    SERVES 4

The Perfect, Fluffy Basmati Rice

INGREDIENTS

- 1.5 cups high-quality aged Basmati rice
- 2 ¼ cups cold water (This is a 1:1.5 rice-to-water ratio)
- 1 teaspoon kosher salt
- Optional Aromatics: 2-3 green cardamom pods, 1-2 whole cloves

Instructions:

- **Rinse:** Place the rice in a large bowl. Cover with water, swirl with your hands, and pour off the milky water. Repeat this 4-5 times, until the water runs mostly clear.

- **Soak:** Cover the rinsed rice with fresh water and let it soak for 30 minutes. This is the most important step for long, fluffy grains.

- **Drain:** Drain the rice completely in a fine-mesh sieve.

- **Cook:** Add the drained rice, the 2 ¼ cups of fresh cold water, salt, and any optional aromatics to a saucepan with a tight-fitting lid.

- **Boil:** Place over high heat and bring to a rolling boil, uncovered.

- **Cover & Simmer:** As soon as it boils, stir it once, turn the heat down to the absolute lowest setting your stove has, and put the lid on tight.

- **Cook:** Let it simmer for 12-15 minutes. Do not lift the lid.

- **Rest:** Turn off the heat completely. Let the pot sit, still covered, for another 10 minutes. This lets the residual steam finish the cooking.

- **Fluff:** Open the lid. You will see small steam-holes on the surface. Use a fork to gently fluff the rice. Serve.

SIMPLIFIED WEEKNIGHT KABULI PULAO

The full, traditional Kabuli Pulao is the national dish of Afghanistan, a masterpiece of meat and rice that can take hours. This is my 30-minute weeknight "cheater's" version. We use pre-cooked chicken (or canned chickpeas) and focus on the three "C's" that define the dish: Carrots, Cumin, and Cardamom.

 PREP 10 MIN    COOK 25 MIN    SERVES 4

Simplified Weeknight Kabuli Pulao

INGREDIENTS

- 1.5 cups Basmati rice, rinsed and soaked
- 1 tablespoon avocado oil
- 2 large carrots, cut into thin matchsticks
- ½ cup raisins or dried currants
- ½ cup slivered almonds
- 1 onion, thinly sliced
- 1 teaspoon Pulao Masala (or: 1 tsp cumin, ½ tsp coriander, ½ tsp cardamom)
- 2 cups cooked, shredded chicken OR 1 (15oz) can of chickpeas, rinsed
- 2 ¼ cups low-sodium chicken or vegetable broth

Instructions:

- Prep Topping: In a large pot or Dutch oven, heat the oil over medium heat. Add the carrot matchsticks and raisins. Sauté for 4-5 minutes until the carrots are soft and the raisins are plump. Use a slotted spoon to remove the carrots and raisins and set them aside.

- Toast Nuts: In the same oil, add the almonds and toast for 1-2 minutes until golden. Remove and set aside.

- Sauté Base: Add the sliced onion to the pot and cook for 5-7 minutes. Add the Pulao Masala (or other spices) and toast for 1 minute.

- Combine: Add the drained rice, the cooked chicken (or chickpeas), and the broth. Stir once.

- Cook: Bring to a boil, then immediately turn the heat to low, cover, and cook for 15 minutes.

- Rest & Serve: Turn off the heat and let it rest, covered, for 10 minutes. Fluff the rice with a fork and transfer to a serving platter. Top with the reserved carrot-raisin mixture and the toasted almonds.

QUINOA PULAO WITH PEAS & CASHEWS

This is the "new" Silk Road. It's my go-to healthy lunch when I want those classic pulao flavors but with a high-protein, gluten-free grain. This one-pot meal comes together in 20 minutes and is a complete, nourishing meal.

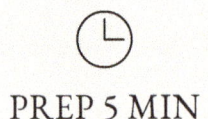

PREP 5 MIN

COOK 20 MIN

SERVES 4

Quinoa Pulao with Peas & Cashews

INGREDIENTS

- 1 tablespoon avocado oil
- 1 teaspoon cumin seeds
- 1 small onion, finely chopped
- 1-inch piece of ginger, grated
- 1 cup tri-color quinoa, rinsed
- ½ teaspoon turmeric powder
- 2 cups vegetable broth
- 1 cup frozen peas
- ½ cup raw, unsalted cashews, toasted
- Fresh cilantro, chopped
- Lemon wedges, for serving

Instructions:

- Sauté Base: In a medium saucepan, heat the oil over medium heat. Add the cumin seeds and toast for 30 seconds. Add the onion and sauté for 4-5 minutes.

- Toast Quinoa: Add the grated ginger and cook for 1 minute. Add the rinsed quinoa and the turmeric. Stir and toast the quinoa for 1-2 minutes.

- Cook: Add the vegetable broth. Bring to a boil, then reduce the heat to low, cover, and simmer for 15 minutes (or until the water is absorbed).

- Rest & Finish: Turn off the heat. Let the pot sit, covered, for 5 minutes.

- Serve: Remove the lid. Add the frozen peas and toasted cashews and fluff the quinoa with a fork. The residual heat will thaw and cook the peas perfectly. Stir in the fresh cilantro and serve with a big squeeze of lemon.

CHAPTER 6

The Radiant Stovetop

(Raitas, Chutneys, Pickles & Quick Breads)

In the West, these are "condiments." In our homes, they are the other half of the meal.

A South Asian, Afghani, or Pakistani meal is never just one note. It is a symphony of contrasting and complementary flavors. A fiery kebab needs a cooling yogurt. A rich, creamy daal needs a sharp, acidic pickle. A soft, hearty curry needs a crunchy salad and a fresh piece of bread to scoop it all up.

This chapter is your toolkit for balance.

These small dishes are the difference between a simple "curry" and a vibrant, exciting meal. They are the bright, tangy, cooling, and crunchy elements that make every bite interesting. The best part? Most of them take five minutes or less, and many can be made days in advance.

Do not skip this chapter. These are not afterthoughts; they are the essential exclamation points that make the whole plate sing.

AVOCADO, MINT & CILANTRO CHUTNEY

This is my modern, healthy take on the classic "green chutney" that is served with everything. Traditionally, green chutney is a watery, spicy-sour sauce. By blending in a whole avocado, we transform it into a creamy, rich, and nutrient-dense dip.

It has all the bright, zesty flavor of the original—the cilantro, mint, ginger, and lime—but with the healthy fats and luxurious body of an avocado. It's a dip, a sauce, and a spread all in one.

PREP 10 MIN

COOK 15 MIN

SERVES 4

Avocado, Mint & Cilantro Chutney

INGREDIENTS

- 1 large ripe avocado, halved and pitted
- 2 cups packed fresh cilantro (stems and all)
- 1 cup packed fresh mint leaves
- 1 green chili (or 2 for more heat)
- 1-inch piece of fresh ginger, peeled
- 1 clove garlic
- Juice of 1 large lime (about 3-4 tablespoons)
- ½ teaspoon ground cumin
- ½ teaspoon kosher salt
- 2-4 tablespoons cold water (to help it blend)

Instructions:

- Prep: Add all the ingredients to a high-speed blender: scoop the avocado in, then add the cilantro, mint, green chili, ginger, garlic, lime juice, cumin, and salt.

- Blend: Add 2 tablespoons of water to start. Blend on high, scraping down the sides as needed, until the chutney is completely smooth and creamy.

- Adjust: If the chutney is too thick to blend, add the remaining water, 1 tablespoon at a time, until it reaches a smooth, dip-like consistency.

- Serve: Taste and adjust for salt or lime juice. Serve immediately.

- To Store: To keep it from browning, press a piece of plastic wrap directly onto the surface of the chutney before covering. It will keep in the fridge for up to 3 days.

SWEET & TANGY DATE AND TAMARIND CHUTNEY

This is the dark, sweet, and sour chutney that is the essential partner to anything crispy—pakoras, bolani, or samosas. Many recipes call for a cup of sugar, but our version gets its body and deep, caramel sweetness entirely from dates.

The tamarind concentrate provides the sourness, and the roasted cumin gives it a smoky, savory backbone. It's an incredibly simple, healthy, and addictive pantry staple.

PREP 10 MIN   COOK 15 MIN   SERVES 4

Sweet & Tangy Date and Tamarind Chutney

INGREDIENTS

- 1 cup (about 150g) pitted Medjool dates
- ½ cup boiling water
- ⅓ cup tamarind concentrate (also called tamarind paste)
- 1 cup cold water
- 1 teaspoon roasted cumin powder
- 1 teaspoon ground ginger
- ½ teaspoon Kashmiri red chili powder
- ½ teaspoon kala namak (black salt) or regular salt

Instructions:

- Soak Dates: Place the pitted dates in a heatproof bowl. Pour the ½ cup of boiling water over them. Let them soak for 30 minutes to soften completely. Do not drain.

- Blend: Transfer the dates and their soaking water to a blender. Add the tamarind concentrate, 1 cup of cold water, roasted cumin, ground ginger, chili powder, and black salt.

- Blend: Blend on high for 60-90 seconds until the mixture is perfectly smooth and silky.

- Adjust: Taste the chutney. It should be a perfect balance of sweet (from the dates) and sour (from the tamarind). If it's too thick, add a splash more water. If it's too tart, add another date and blend again.

- Serve: Serve as a dipping sauce. It will keep in an airtight jar in the refrigerator for up to two weeks.

CUCUMBER & CUMIN RAITA (THE COOLING CLASSIC)

This is the ultimate fire extinguisher for spicy food. The cooling properties of the yogurt and cucumber instantly soothe the palate, while the roasted cumin (the most important ingredient) adds a toasty, nutty, and savory depth. It takes two minutes to make and is non-negotiable alongside kebabs, pulao, or any spicy curry.

PREP 5 MIN

COOK 15 MIN

SERVES 4

Cucumber & Cumin Raita (The Cooling Classic)

INGREDIENTS

- 1.5 cups plain Greek yogurt (or plain whole-milk yogurt)
- ½ English cucumber, grated
- ½ teaspoon roasted cumin powder (this is essential)
- ¼ teaspoon kosher salt
- ¼ teaspoon ground black pepper
- 1 tablespoon fresh cilantro or mint, finely chopped (optional)

Instructions:

- Prep Cucumber: Grate the cucumber on the large holes of a box grater. The secret: Squeeze the grated cucumber in your fist over the sink to remove all the excess water. This prevents a watery raita.

- Mix: In a medium bowl, combine the Greek yogurt, the squeezed cucumber, the roasted cumin powder, salt, and pepper.

- Serve: Stir to combine. Garnish with the fresh herbs (if using) and an extra sprinkle of roasted cumin. Serve cold.

AFGHANI 'CHAKKAH' (STRAINED GARLIC & MINT YOGURT)

If raita is the cooling, soupy side dish, Chakkah is its bold, thick, and intense cousin. This is the classic Afghani yogurt dip served with Bolani (Chapter 3) and Banjan Borani (Chapter 3). It's essentially homemade Greek yogurt, punched up with a sharp, raw garlic kick and the coolness of dried mint.

PREP 5 MIN   COOK 15 MIN   SERVES 4

Afghani 'Chakkah'
(Strained Garlic & Mint Yogurt)

INGREDIENTS

- 1.5 cups plain Greek yogurt
- 1-2 cloves garlic, pressed or grated to a fine paste
- 1 teaspoon dried mint, crushed between your palms
- ½ teaspoon kosher salt

Instructions:

- Mix: In a small bowl, combine the Greek yogurt, the grated garlic paste, the crushed dried mint, and the salt.

- Infuse: Stir vigorously to combine. For the best flavor, let it sit in the fridge for at least 15 minutes to allow the garlic and mint flavors to infuse the yogurt.

- Serve: Serve as a thick dip for kebabs or a spread for flatbread.

SIRKE WAALE PYAAZ
(QUICK-PICKLED VINEGAR ONIONS)

This is that bright-pink, crunchy, and tangy onion salad you get at the best Indian restaurants. It's the perfect, sharp counterpoint to rich, heavy dishes like Daal Makhani or Nihari. This is not a "canning" recipe; it's a 10-minute "quick pickle" that you make and store in the fridge.

 PREP 10 MIN    COOK 15 MIN    SERVES 4

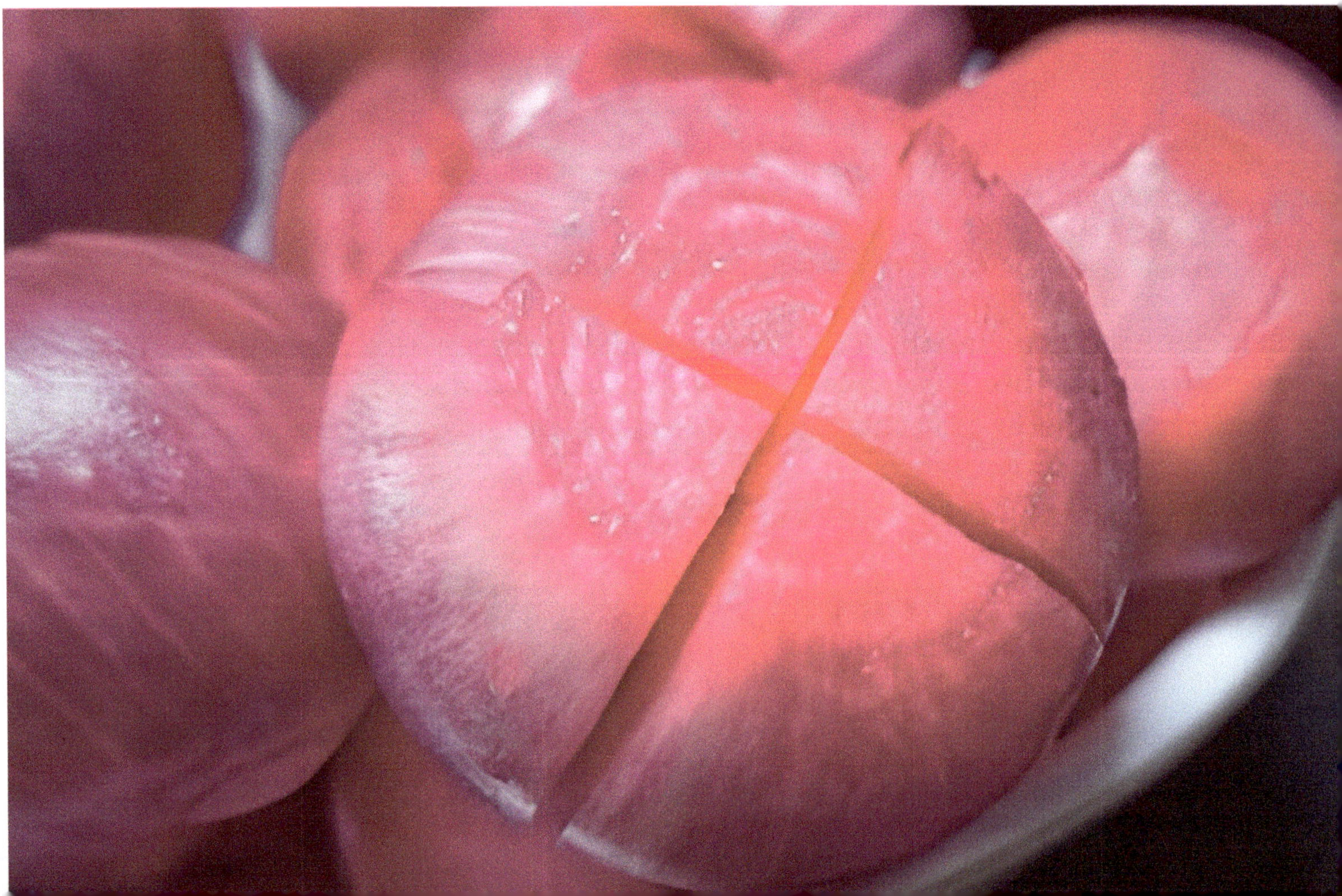

Sirke Waale Pyaaz
(Quick-Pickled Vinegar Onions)

INGREDIENTS

- 1 large red onion, thinly sliced into rings
- 1 small chunk of beetroot (about 1-inch), peeled (this is the secret to the pink color!)
- 1-2 green chilies, slit lengthwise (optional)
- ½ cup white vinegar
- ½ cup hot water
- 1 tablespoon honey or maple syrup
- 1.5 teaspoons kosher salt

Instructions:

- Pack Jar: In a clean glass jar (like a mason jar), pack in the sliced red onion, the small chunk of beetroot, and the green chilies (if using).

- Make Brine: In a small bowl, whisk together the white vinegar, hot water, honey, and salt until the salt and honey are completely dissolved.

- Pour & Wait: Pour the brine over the onions in the jar. Press the onions down to make sure they are submerged.

- Serve: Seal the jar. You can serve them after just 30 minutes, but they are best after 2-3 hours, when they've turned a brilliant, electric pink. They will keep in the fridge for up to two weeks.

SIMPLE WHOLE-WHEAT ROTI (THE EVERYDAY BREAD)

In our homes, naan (which is leavened and often made with white flour) is for parties and restaurants. Roti (also called chapati) is for every day. This is our humble, healthy, unleavened, whole-wheat bread. It's the essential, nutritious vehicle for scooping up every daal and sabzi in this book. It's just flour, water, and salt.

PREP 10 MIN   **COOK 20 MIN**   **SERVES 4**

Simple Whole-Wheat Roti
(The Everyday Bread)

INGREDIENTS

- 2 cups atta (whole-wheat durum flour) (see note)
- 1 teaspoon kosher salt
- 1 teaspoon avocado or olive oil (optional, for softness)
- ~¾ cup warm water
- Note: Atta is a very finely milled whole-wheat flour. You can find it at any South Asian grocery or online. In a pinch, regular whole-wheat flour will work, but the texture will be different.

Instructions:

- Make Dough: In a large bowl, whisk together the atta and salt. Add the optional oil. Slowly pour in the warm water as you mix with your other hand, until a shaggy, soft (but not sticky) dough comes together.

- Knead: Turn the dough out onto a clean counter and knead for 5-7 minutes until it is smooth and elastic.

- Rest: Place the dough back in the bowl, cover with a damp cloth, and let it rest for at least 20 minutes. This is crucial for a soft roti.

- Divide & Roll: Divide the dough into 8 equal-sized balls. On a lightly floured surface, take one ball and roll it out into a thin, even circle (about 6-7 inches wide).

- Cook (Part 1): Heat a dry tawa (a flat griddle) or a cast-iron skillet over medium-high heat. Place the rolled-out roti on the hot pan. Cook for 30-45 seconds, until you see small bubbles form on the surface.

- Cook (Part 2): Flip the roti. Cook on the other side for about 1 minute, until you see small brown spots.

- Puff (The Magic): This is the final step. Using tongs, carefully lift the roti off the pan and place it directly on the open flame of your gas burner. In seconds, it should magically puff up into a beautiful ball. Flip it once, quickly, then remove.

- No Gas Flame? No problem. Instead of the flame, press down on the roti in the pan with a clean kitchen towel. Pressing the edges will encourage it to puff up in the pan.

- Serve: Transfer the hot roti to a plate and (traditionally) brush it with a tiny bit of ghee or oil. Stack them and keep them wrapped in a cloth to stay warm.

CHAPTER 7

Light & Fragrant Sweets

(Healthy Desserts for the Modern Kitchen)

In my family, no celebration—in fact, no meal of any importance—is complete without something sweet, a meetha.

Traditional desserts from India, Pakistan, and Afghanistan are legendary. They are also unapologetically indulgent: deep-fried jalebis soaked in syrup, rich, dense barfis made with cups of sugar and ghee, and creamy kheer (rice pudding) slowly simmered with full-fat milk and sugar.

I adore these desserts. I also know I can't eat them every day.

This chapter is my answer to the question: "How can I have a sweet, fragrant, and satisfying end to my meal that doesn't undo all my healthy choices?"

These are my "new" sweets. They are light, built on natural sweeteners like dates, honey, and mangoes, and infused with the royal fragrances of our heritage—saffron, cardamom, and rose water. We skip the deep-fryer for the air fryer, swap heavy cream for coconut milk and chia seeds, and find that we can create desserts that are just as complex and celebratory as the classics.

This is sweetness, reimagined.

SAFFRON & CARDAMOM PANNA COTTA (WITH AGAR-AGAR)

This is a beautiful, elegant dessert that proves "healthy" can also be "luxurious." Panna Cotta (Italian for "cooked cream") is a simple, set pudding. My version is lighter, using a mix of coconut milk and regular milk (or all coconut milk to make it dairy-free) and sweetened with honey.

We set it with agar-agar, a natural, plant-based gelatin derived from seaweed. The result is a silky, jiggly, and creamy pudding that is the perfect canvas for our most royal flavors: saffron and cardamom.

PREP 10 MIN	COOK 15 MIN	SERVES 4

Saffron & Cardamom Panna Cotta (with Agar-Agar)

INGREDIENTS

- 1 (14oz) can full-fat coconut milk
- 1 cup milk (almond, oat, or dairy)
- ¼ cup honey or maple syrup (or to taste)
- 1 large pinch of high-quality saffron threads
- ½ teaspoon ground cardamom
- 2 teaspoons agar-agar powder
- Garnish: Crushed pistachios and dried rose petals

Instructions:

- **Infuse:** In a small saucepan, gently warm the coconut milk and regular milk over medium-low heat. Add the honey, saffron threads, and ground cardamom. Whisk until the honey is dissolved. Let it steep for 5 minutes (do not let it boil).

- **Activate Agar:** In a small, separate bowl, whisk the agar-agar powder with ¼ cup of cold water until it's a smooth slurry.

- **Combine & Boil:** Pour the agar-agar slurry into the warm milk mixture. Now, turn the heat up to medium and bring the mixture to a full, rolling boil, whisking constantly.

- **Simmer:** As soon as it boils, reduce the heat and simmer gently for 2 minutes, whisking the whole time. This step is essential to activate the agar.

- **Pour & Set:** Turn off the heat. Divide the mixture among four small ramekins or dessert glasses.

- **Chill:** Let them cool on the counter for 20 minutes, then transfer to the refrigerator to chill for at least 4 hours, or until completely firm.

- **Serve:** To serve, you can unmold them onto a plate or just serve them in their glasses, garnished with a sprinkle of crushed pistachios and dried rose petals.

AIR FRYER 'SHAHI TUKDA' (CRISPED BREAD IN SAFFRON MILK)

Shahi Tukda, or "Royal Morsel," is a decadent Mughal dessert made of bread deep-fried in ghee, soaked in sugar syrup, and then topped with a thickened, sweetened milk cream called rabri. It is absolutely incredible, and incredibly heavy.

This is my air fryer hack. We get the bread perfectly golden and crispy with just a light spray of oil. And we swap the heavy rabri for a quick, light, and fragrant saffron-almond milk that soaks into the bread just beautifully. It's the royal dessert, fit for a weeknight.

PREP 15 MIN   COOK 10 MIN   SERVES 4

Air Fryer 'Shahi Tukda' (Crisped Bread in Saffron Milk)

INGREDIENTS

- 4 thick slices of day-old bread (brioche, challah, or simple white bread), crusts removed
- Avocado oil spray
- 2 cups milk (I use unsweetened almond milk)
- 1 large pinch of saffron threads
- ¼ teaspoon ground cardamom
- 2 tablespoons honey or maple syrup
- 2 tablespoons slivered almonds, toasted
- 2 tablespoons chopped pistachios

Instructions:

- **Crisp Bread:** Cut each slice of bread diagonally into two triangles. Preheat your air fryer to 380°F (190°C).

- **Air Fry:** Spray the bread triangles on all sides with oil. Place them in the air fryer basket in a single layer (work in batches). Air fry for 5-8 minutes, flipping halfway, until they are deep golden brown and very crispy, like a giant crouton.

- **Make Milk:** While the bread is in the fryer, heat the almond milk, saffron, and cardamom in a small saucepan over medium heat. Let it come to a gentle simmer (do not boil). Stir in the honey or maple syrup until dissolved.

- **Assemble:** Arrange the crispy, hot bread triangles on a serving platter.

- **Serve:** Pour the hot saffron milk slowly over the bread. Let it soak in for 1-2 minutes. Garnish generously with the toasted almonds and chopped pistachios and serve immediately, while the bread is still warm and crispy in parts.

DATE & FIG 'LADDOO' (5-MINUTE ENERGY BALLS)

A laddoo is a traditional, ball-shaped Indian sweet. My "new" laddoos are the perfect, healthy, 5-minute treat. They use the natural, caramel-like sweetness of dates and figs, the healthy fats of almonds and cashews, and the warm, fragrant spice of cardamom.

These are my go-to for an after-dinner sweet craving, a pre-workout energy boost, or a healthy snack for my kids' lunchboxes.

PREP 10 MIN   COOK 15 MIN   SERVES 4

Date & Fig 'Laddoo' (5-Minute Energy Balls)

INGREDIENTS

- 1 cup (about 150g) pitted Medjool dates
- ½ cup dried figs (like Calimyrna or Mission)
- ½ cup raw, unsalted almonds
- ½ cup raw, unsalted cashews or walnuts
- 1 tablespoon chia seeds or flax seeds (optional)
- ½ teaspoon ground cardamom
- 1 pinch of sea salt
- For Rolling: 2-3 tablespoons toasted sesame seeds or desiccated coconut

Instructions:

- Pulse Nuts: In a food processor, add the almonds and cashews. Pulse 10-12 times until they are broken down into a coarse, pebbly meal.

- Combine: Add the pitted dates, dried figs, chia seeds (if using), cardamom, and salt.

- Blend: Run the food processor for 1-2 minutes continuously. The mixture will look crumbly at first, but then the "dough" will suddenly come together into a large, sticky ball.

- Roll: Place your rolling ingredient (sesame seeds or coconut) on a small plate. Take about 1 tablespoon of the date mixture and roll it between your palms to form a smooth ball.

- Coat: Roll the ball in the sesame seeds to coat. Set on a plate and repeat with the remaining mixture.

- Serve: You can eat them immediately. They will firm up in the refrigerator and can be stored in an airtight container in the fridge for up to 2 weeks.

ROSE WATER & PISTACHIO 'NICE CREAM'

"Nice Cream" is the internet's name for a brilliant hack: a creamy, dairy-free "ice cream" made entirely from frozen bananas. Because it's so simple, it's the perfect canvas for our elegant Silk Road flavors. The rose water and pistachio instantly transport this modern health-food to the courtyards of Persia.

PREP 5 MIN

COOK 15 MIN

SERVES 2-3

Rose Water & Pistachio 'Nice Cream'

INGREDIENTS

- 3 large, very ripe bananas, peeled, sliced, and frozen solid
- 1 teaspoon pure rose water
- ½ teaspoon ground cardamom
- 2 tablespoons unsweetened almond milk (or just enough to get it to blend)
- ⅓ cup shelled pistachios, roughly chopped (plus extra for garnish)
- 1 tablespoon dried rose petals (optional, for garnish)

Instructions:

- Blend: Place the frozen banana slices in a high-speed blender or a food processor. Add the rose water, cardamom, and 2 tablespoons of almond milk.

- Blend: Blend on high, using the blender's tamper (or stopping to scrape down the sides) to push the bananas into the blades. It will look crumbly at first, but suddenly it will whip into a thick, smooth, soft-serve ice cream consistency.

- Fold-In: Add the ⅓ cup of chopped pistachios and pulse just 2-3 times to mix them in. Do not over-blend, or you'll lose the crunchy texture.

- Serve: For a "soft-serve" consistency, spoon it directly into bowls. Garnish with more pistachios and the dried rose petals.

- For Hard-Pack: For a firmer, scoop-able ice cream, transfer the mixture to a loaf pan, cover, and freeze for at least 2 hours.

MANGO & COCONUT CHIA SEED PUDDING

This is my healthy answer to a mango kheer or mango fool. Chia seeds are a superfood, and when they soak in liquid, they create a wonderful, thick, tapioca-like pudding. We layer this simple pudding with a vibrant, naturally sweet mango purée and infuse it with cardamom. It's a breakfast, a snack, and a dessert all in one.

PREP 10 MIN

COOK 15 MIN

SERVES 2

Mango & Coconut Chia Seed Pudding

INGREDIENTS

- ¼ cup black chia seeds
- 1 cup lite coconut milk (from a can)
- 1 tablespoon maple syrup or honey
- ½ teaspoon ground cardamom
- 1 large, very ripe mango, peeled and chopped
- 1 teaspoon lime juice
- Garnish: Toasted coconut flakes and fresh mint

Instructions:

- Make Pudding: In a medium bowl or jar, whisk together the chia seeds, coconut milk, maple syrup, and ground cardamom.

- Set: Let it sit for 5 minutes, then whisk again (this prevents clumping). Cover and place in the refrigerator for at least 2 hours, or overnight, until it's thick and set.

- Make Purée: While the pudding is setting, add the chopped mango and the lime juice to a small blender. Blend until perfectly smooth.

- Assemble: Get two serving glasses. Create layers: a layer of the chia pudding, followed by a layer of the mango purée. Repeat until the glasses are full.

- Serve: Garnish with a sprinkle of toasted coconut flakes and a fresh mint leaf.

ALMOND-FLOUR BESAN BARFI
(A HEALTHY-ISH TREAT)

A true barfi is a dense, milk- or flour-based fudge, and Besan Barfi (made from chickpea flour) is a nutty classic. This is my quick, "healthy-ish" version.

By using a blend of almond flour and chickpea flour (besan), we get a rich, nutty, high-protein base. We toast it in just a little bit of avocado oil (or ghee if you're feeling it) and sweeten it with maple syrup. It's a quick, gluten-free, and deeply satisfying treat that comes together in 15 minutes.

 PREP 5 MIN    COOK 15 MIN    SERVES 4

Almond-Flour Besan Barfi
(A Healthy-ish Treat)

INGREDIENTS

- 1 cup almond flour
- ½ cup chickpea flour (besan)
- 3 tablespoons avocado oil (or ghee)
- ½ teaspoon ground cardamom
- ⅓ cup maple syrup
- Garnish: Slivered almonds or pistachios

Instructions:

- Line Pan: Line a small square pan or a loaf pan with parchment paper.

- Toast Flours: In a non-stick skillet over medium-low heat, add the avocado oil, almond flour, and chickpea flour.

- Stir: Cook, stirring constantly (this is a "roasting" step), for 10-12 minutes. The flours will become fragrant, nutty, and turn a light golden brown. Do not walk away, as they can burn quickly.

- Combine: Turn off the heat. Stir in the ground cardamom. Let it cool for 1 minute.

- Sweeten: Pour in the maple syrup and stir vigorously. The mixture will instantly thicken and pull away from the sides of the pan.

- Press & Set: Immediately transfer the mixture to your lined pan. Use the back of a spoon (or your hands, covered in parchment) to press it down into a flat, even layer. Sprinkle the top with slivered almonds.

- Serve: Let it cool completely on the counter for 1 hour (or in the fridge for 20 minutes) to set. Once firm, use the parchment paper to lift the barfi out and cut it into small squares.

Acknowledgements
(A Note of Thanks)

This book, like every meal I've ever cooked, was not a solo effort. It is the product of a thousand conversations, a hundred borrowed ideas, and an immeasurable amount of love and patience from the people in my life.

My deepest thanks go to my family, who have been the most loving and honest recipe testers a writer could ask for. To my Ammi and Abbu, who patiently answered my endless, frantic calls: "How much anardana? Are you sure you don't measure the ginger? What does 'cook until it's done' mean?" Thank you for sharing your kitchen wisdom with me.

To my Daadi and Naani, who are no longer with us. I hope I have done justice to your flavors. This book is my love letter to you.

To my partner, who ate more chapli kebab test batches than anyone should have to, and who washed the (many, many) dishes, even when the recipes went horribly wrong. I could not have done this without you.

To my children, who now ask for "pink chai" and "crispy pakoras" by name. You are my inspiration for keeping this heritage alive, in a healthy, vibrant way.

And finally, to you, the reader. Thank you for welcoming me into your kitchen. I hope these recipes bring you a fraction of the joy, comfort, and connection that they have brought me.

May your pantry be full and your table always be shared.

With gratitude,

Zara Mustafa

A Note on Sourcing

Many of the ingredients that give these recipes their authentic "magic" may be new to you.

Don't be intimidated! Twenty years ago, they required a special trip; today, almost all of them can be found online or in larger supermarkets.

- Your Best Friend: Your local Indian, Pakistani, or Middle Eastern grocery store is your greatest resource. The owners are often incredibly knowledgeable and can point you to the best brands.

- Atta (Whole-Wheat Flour): Look for finely milled, whole-wheat durum flour. Popular brands include "Suhani" or "Chakki Gold."

- Anardana (Dried Pomegranate Seeds): You can find these whole or pre-ground. They are essential for that chapli kebab tang.

- Kasoori Methi (Dried Fenugreek Leaves): Do not skip this. It's the "restaurant-style" secret. It's sold in boxes and is very inexpensive.

- Kala Namak (Black Salt): This pinkish-grey, sulfurous salt adds a funky, savory depth to raita and our Khyber Cooler.

- Amchur (Dried Mango Powder): Your go-to for a bright, fruity sourness.

- Tamarind Concentrate: Look for a dark, thick paste in a jar, often from Thailand or India. It lasts forever in the fridge.

- Kashmiri Red Chili Powder: This is my non-negotiable for bright color without fiery heat.

www.ingramcontent.com/pod-product-compliance
Lightning Source LLC
Chambersburg PA
CBHW061127070526
44584CB00033B/4246